THE BOOK OF
WOODEN BOATS

THE BOOK OF
WOODEN BOATS

Photographs by Benjamin Mendlowitz

Text by Maynard Bray

W. W. NORTON & COMPANY

NEW YORK • LONDON

For Deborah and Anne

Other books of photography by Benjamin Mendlowitz:
Wood, Water & Light
A Passage in Time

The text of this book is composed in Goudy
Book design by Sherry Streeter, Brooklin, Maine
Production by NOAH Publications, Brooklin, Maine
Imagesetting by High Resolution, Camden, Maine
Printed by Dai Nippon Printing Co., Japan

First Edition

Library of Congress Cataloging-in-Publication Data

Mendlowitz, Benjamin
    The book of wooden boats / photographs by Benjamin Mendlowitz:
text by Maynard Bray.
        p.   cm.
    Includes index.
    ISBN 0-393-03417-8
    1. Wooden boats. 2. Wooden boats—United States. 3. Ships.
Wooden. 4. Ships, Wooden—United States.   I. Bray, Maynard.

II. Title
VM321.M45   1992
623.8'207—dc20

ISBN 0-393-03417-8

W.W. Norton & Company, Inc., 500 Fifth Avenue, New York, N.Y.
W.W. Norton & Company, LTD., 10 Coptic Street, London WCIA IPU

1 2 3 4 5 6 7 8 9 0

CONTENTS

III. WORKING BOATS

IV. OPEN BOATS

V. SAILING YACHTS

FOREWORD

Many of the photographs in this book were originally published in the *Calendar of Wooden Boats*. In fact, the *Calendar*'s having passed the 10-year mark—a genuine achievement for a publication of that nature—provided the inspiration for the book.

Most calendars are treated shabbily. Featuring hackneyed photographs of wide-eyed kittens playing with balls of yarn or of sway-backed covered bridges in the New England countryside, they are given away indiscriminately by auto-parts dealers and insurance brokers. They are sold in gift shops and variety stores alongside giant economy rolls of holiday wrapping paper and packages of chewing gum. They are published to be consumed. Their users tack them to the wall at the beginning of the year, scribble notes on them daily, rip a page off monthly, and throw away the carcasses at the end of the year. *Sic transit gloria mundi.*

But every once in a while a special calendar appears that, by its very nature, cannot be so treated. Yes, it will be hung on the wall, and yes, it will be used to track daily engagements, but it will not be mutilated during the course of the year and it will not be discarded when its time has run out. Rather, it will be admired and savored, and at the end of the year it will be saved. Its images will be too original, too powerful, to be thrown out with the last of the holiday beer bottles.

For 10 years now the *Calendar of Wooden Boats*, which this book celebrates, has been such a special calendar. Replaced annually with a new edition but never retired, the *Calendar of Wooden Boats* is one of those memorable documents that encompasses an era, not a single year.

The first *Calendar of Wooden Boats* was published in 1983. Few observers then gave it much chance of success. It was about boats hand-crafted of wood at a time when the vast majority were being factory-produced in plastic. It was about old-style design at a time when traditionalism seemed at its nadir and modernism at its height. It was about boats in a country that seemed to have turned its back on the sea. It was for sale for real money, not given away wholesale as an advertising premium. It was relatively expensive and difficult to find, with no mass-market distribution. It was published at the end of a dirt road in Maine, not in New York City. Its images were by a photographer whose name may have been reasonably well known by wooden-boat aficionados, but was hardly a household word in the rest of America. Yet despite those drawbacks, the calendar quickly developed an ardent following, so much so that it is now one of the premier art calendars published in the country today.

Why? My guess is that most people instantly recognize, and are touched by, its symbolism. Whether we are boat lovers or not, the *Calendar of Wooden Boats* tells us through powerful images that the best of the past can be maintained in the present and that what may seem to be disposable now need not be that way in the future. Like the wooden boats it features, the calendar is a metaphor for excellence in a world that all too often settles for less.

The *Calendar of Wooden Boats* was conceived by Benjamin Mendlowitz, a professional photographer who has specialized in the marine field since the late 1970s. Born and bred in New York City, he attended Brandeis University, where he majored in physics and concentrated in film. Following college, he traveled in Europe and then moved to Boston, where he worked for a producer of training-film strips. Five years later, without a specialty, he quit his full-time job and went out on the road as a free-lance photographer.

In the course of an assignment on Mount Desert Island in Maine, Mendlowitz met Jonathan Wilson, publisher of *WoodenBoat* magazine, and his associate Maynard Bray. *WoodenBoat* was a relatively new magazine—a phenomenon, in fact—at the forefront of a renascent interest in traditional watercraft. At the time Mendlowitz had been photographing boats, which he had been fascinated by since his youth, but only as a sideline to his regular work. But Wilson and Bray recognized Mendlowitz's talent and encouraged him to concentrate on the craft that seemed to be fast disappearing. Few professional marine photographers were paying attention to wooden watercraft. Most were concentrating on modern boats and yachts. That, after all, was where the money was.

Mendlowitz was in the right place at the right time. Jonathan Wilson and Maynard Bray were looking for a photographer who had an appreciation for wooden boats and the ability to capture their essence on film. Mendlowitz was looking for a specialty. And so began a collaboration, especially with Bray, who was to provide considerable advice, that would result in a continuing series of photographs that would rival—and in some ways surpass—the work of the great marine photographers of the past. Eventually, Mendlowitz's work would appear beyond the pages of *WoodenBoat* magazine: in most of the major yachting magazines here and abroad, in *Connoisseur*, the *New York Times Magazine*, *Yankee*, *Historic Preservation*; and in the books *Wood, Water, & Light* and *A Passage in Time*; and, of course, in the *Calendar of Wooden Boats*.

What makes the work of Benjamin Mendlowitz so much different from that of other boating photographers? There are many answers, but an acquired passion for the subject would have to be at the top of the list, followed closely by attention to detail, an understanding of the nature of light, the eye of an artist, technical mastery, and the ability to reveal the essence of a boat's soul.

Careful study of the photographs in this book will reveal some or all of the these elements. But to my mind not one is more representative of Mendlowitz's technical skill, artistic interpretation, aesthetics, and appreciation of the classical past than the photograph of the Nutshell pram and Downeast peapod on page 148. What a beautiful, elegant, eloquent portrait of two unpretentious small boats at peace by the edge of the sea!

It is a gentle summer evening on the coast of Maine. A full moon is rising over a spit of sand joining two islands at low tide near the eastern end of Eggemoggin Reach. The water is reflecting the deep purple sky. The scene is split horizontally by the sand spit, vertically by a line of gold thrown by the moon. Two boats—one rigged for sail, with a red streamer extended by a zephyr; the other a double-ended rowboat with a blue sheerstrake—are visually joined by the sand and, at the same time, split by the gold line. It is a perfectly composed image that on the one hand could be called a portrait of two boats and on the other could be called a portrait of the coast with two boats as accents.

The photograph reeks of the Benjamin Mendlowitz aesthetic. There is no time; it could be now, it could be then, it could be whenever the viewer wants it to be. There is no out-of-context background, no distortion from an unnatural lens, no photographic gimmickry, no distracting debris left behind by the owners of the boats. There are, in fact, no boat owners in sight. Whose boats are these? Someone else's? Maybe, but then again, they could be ours.

Our boats, our coast, our scene. We are no longer looking at a photograph. We are looking into a scene; we are in a scene; it is our scene; we are there. That is what makes a photograph by Benjamin Mendlowitz different from all the others.

Peter H. Spectre
Camden, Maine

INTRODUCTION

A book is among the more long-lasting of modern man's creations, and there is little doubt that this book will be around far longer than the majority of the boats shown on its pages. And, although the calendars from which many of these images come have that same potential, neither libraries nor other archival institutions are generally set up to handle such aberrations from the classic hardcover bound imprints that we call books. Thus, it pleases me greatly that, with this publication, Benjamin Mendlowitz's beautiful photographs of beautiful boats will be conveniently available for many years to come.

The boats themselves I fear are another matter. Wooden boats—especially the larger yachts—are a valuable heritage in peril. Few new ones are being built, and too many old ones are crumbling from neglect. Revealing the greatness of these craft by means of photographs has been a major objective of the *Calendar of Wooden Boats* for the last decade, and it is our hope that in some small way we have helped to slow the rate of attrition—and, perhaps, have even encouraged the construction of new wooden boats. This book, which contains most of those calendar selections and adds to the coverage of many of the boats previously featured, simply underscores that hope.

How the calendars, and now this book, are produced might be of interest. Focusing on boats that are good is important, if the presentation is to be evocative, but equally vital are the quality of the photographs, the background color selection, and the printing. It has been my good fortune to have worked closely with Benjamin Mendlowitz since he started this endeavor back in 1983, and I can say without reservation that quality accompanies every step in the production process.

Take the printing, for example. Benjamin and calendar and book designer Sherry Streeter every year have been right there at press time, on call round the clock to check that the colors are correct and that the work is up to their high standards. The results, I know, speak for themselves.

The pictures are good because Benjamin is an incredible photographer, one who has the energy and good judgment to be in the right place at the right time, a marvelous eye for color and composition, and the dexterity needed to manipulate a couple of cameras when the action is fast, the footing is shaky, and salt spray lands on the lens—and has to be wiped off—with every wave.

Credit the attractive design of this book to the same talent who does the calendar: Sherry Streeter.

As for myself, besides doing the writing, I have been involved to varying degrees in selecting the boats that Benjamin has photographed, and I have worked at times to "set up" the photographs by driving the photo boats from which Benjamin shoots. (Those have been various, and well worth a lampoon edition of the calendar: from greasy runabouts to 60' patrol boats manned by uniformed crews, to tiny rubber rafts, to classic gasoline launches where makeshift steering saved the "take.") Every year, 12 pictures are selected during several end-of-the-season showings where Benjamin, Sherry, and I, along with some family and a few well-chosen friends, view several hundred candidates, then finally close in—not without considerable politicking. Sherry's fine eye for color, impact, and overall composition comes into play, while Benjamin always watches for good skies and lighting and, of course, technical excellence; I concentrate on the boats themselves.

The boats in and around Brooklin, Maine, where we live could easily adorn calendars for the next 10 years, and they have, in fact, made up the greatest single body of photographs used over the last decade. But we try, as we shoot and select, to provide as wide a geographic spread as possible. We also try to give a fair share of exposure to boats large and small, pleasure and commercial, sail and power, old and new— along with boatshops, close-ups, and interiors. With the additional space available in this book, we have been able to include other views of many of the boats to help with your understanding and appreciation of them.

In spite of the creative imaging technology that's available for "improving" photographs, none of Benjamin's ever get any kind of retouching or any other manipulation. They are all natural just as they appear in the original slides, and for this reason, the boats have to look just about perfect as they are being shot. They can't be towing ugly dinghies, or displaying slack halyards or lines dragging over the side or a motley crowd on deck. Thus, it occasionally takes a little time to "set up" some boats. We might, for example, tow their dinghy behind our photo boat, then ask half the crew to get out of sight below. If the boat has a list to starboard, the crew might even have to sit on the port side below to compensate. But this kind of fussing is what makes good pictures as well as good boats. We hope you enjoy the results.

Maynard Bray
Brooklin, Maine

ACKNOWLEDGMENTS

In the early years of the *Calendar of Wooden Boats*, all the images came from my magazine assignment work with *WoodenBoat*, *Sail*, and *Nautical Quarterly*. As I was encouraged to publish the calendar by *WoodenBoat*'s Jon Wilson and Terry Driscoll, one of my objectives was to give people a chance to see some of the other images from these assignments. It was great fun to go back through the files looking for our favorite shots, without the constraint of having to choose an image to tell or illustrate a story.

As a photographer, I would simply want to select the 12 photographs that were the most visually dramatic, those shots that I had worked hardest to get and knew could never be repeated because of the unique, if not magical, combination of wind, sea, sky, and light. Fortunately, I was not left entirely on my own. Maynard Bray was a collaborator from the first and, although he is an artist and photographer with keen visual instincts, his first love and his driving devotion is to the boats themselves. So if a shot with a spectacular sky was of a mediocre boat it would not be included; if there was a dramatic image of a fine boat that was poorly maintained, carrying an odd sail combination, or whose sails were poorly trimmed it would be passed over for one in which everything was right to the true mariner's eye. Thus looking back on the first 10 years of the calendar, we had not simply a collection of pretty shots, but images of some of the finest remaining wooden boats in existence, properly maintained, rigged, and sailed.

Jim Mairs, my editor at W. W. Norton and a sailor himself, recognized this collection and became the trigger for pulling together in this book our favorite images from the calendar. And like the early years of the calendar, this book afforded us the chance to share some additional images of these fine boats that were taken on assignment or created specifically for the calendar, but for one reason or another have until now remained hidden in my files. It also gave me the opportunity to work on another project with graphic artist Sherry Streeter, whose innovative and stunning design for the calendar has complemented and enhanced my photographs just as a finely crafted frame gives added dimension to a painting.

So, I have taken this space to tell you a bit about how the calendar and this book came into being, but more importantly to thank those people mentioned above as well as all those who provided encouragement, inspiration, and help along the way including: Deborah Brewster, Anne Bray, Kathy Brandes, Claire Cramer, Joe Gribbins, Will Holloway, Louie Howland, Milton and Muriel Mendlowitz, Marty Pedersen, Eleanor Rhinelander, Peter Spectre, and David Westphal. My appreciation extends to all of you along with the countless boatbuilders, boat owners, and sailors who allowed me to photograph them and their craft and went to the extra effort to make that special shot possible.

Benjamin Mendlowitz
Brooklin, Maine

THE BOOK OF
WOODEN BOATS

CHAPTER I

SAILBOATS

The sailing craft shown in this chapter are the cruisers and racers under 40' and craft, such as Cape Cod catboats, with traditional workboat ancestry. These are the boats that most of us identify with and many of us own, a type that has been around for over a century and has given great pleasure to owners and observers alike. Usually sailed and cared for by their owners, and usually moved by the wind alone, they are thought of as being among the more practical of pleasure craft. I'm convinced that size has little to do with absolute beauty, and you'll find that these sailboats can hold their own with the larger and generally fancier craft that can be found in the chapter entitled "Sailing Yachts."

Able is typical of what we have categorized as sailboats. Here, with the Olympic mountain range in the distance, this neat little cutter heads out across the Strait of Juan de Fuca, and home to Port Townsend, Washington. She's out of wind just now, and a sculling oar over the stern moves her along ever so quietly. She's being carried by the current as well and, in fact, her early-morning start was timed to catch the very first of the favoring flood tide. Today, in this her first year afloat (1984), she leaves the annual Victoria Classic Boat Festival with a most significant prize—Best Sailboat Overall. Her owner-builder has good reason to feel proud.

Able represents what is so special about a wooden boat. A person can start out with little more than a good design and a pile of lumber, and in time, with careful work and a moderate amount of money, create an object of true quality—complimented wherever she goes, yet useful for everyday sailing and cruising as well.

ABLE, an owner-built cutter   LOA: 24'0"   Beam: 8'11"   Designed by Lyle Hess   Built 1984 by Bertram Levy, Port Townsend, Washington   Photographed off Victoria, British Columbia, Canada

BRYONY

An English-style cutter built in Port Townsend

As her name suggests, *Bryony* (meaning a small flowering plant of English origin that's good for what ails you) has roots in the British Isles. Armed with photographs of plumb-stemmed single-stickers of Britain's Cornish coast, Frank and Kitty Reithel visited The Northwest School of Wooden Boatbuilding in Port Townsend, Washington, where they commissioned the designing and building of a cutter with that kind of style and rig. Then both Reithels promptly enrolled as students so they could put the skills they would be learning into practice on this new boat of theirs right from the beginning. The scheme worked perfectly. In 18 months, they had their boat (except for the interior, which they built after launching), plus all the help they wanted for sailing it.

Three days after Christmas in 1990, *Bryony* came ashore when her berth at the Hadlock, Washington, marina broke up in hurricane-force northerly winds. The hull, although holed, was saved, but the rig was lost. By the time you read this, however, *Bryony* will have been repaired at the school where she was built and will look, once again, just as she does in these photographs.

LOA: 34'0"   Beam: 10'0"
Designed by Jim Franken
*Built 1983 by The Northwest School of Wooden
    Boatbuilding, Port Townsend, Washington*
Photographed off Hadlock, Washington

ANNIE

A new boat built to an old design

The economic depression between 1929 and World War II started a "small is beautiful" movement and caused a number of yacht designers to look toward tabloid cruisers as a means of survival during those lean years. *Annie* is such a design, drawn " on speculation" in 1932 by Fenwick Williams, and is what one might call a successful transition from a workboat since Williams based her on several of his favorite commercial sailing craft. Her hull is truly handsome, and her exceptionally well-modeled bow and stern come from a sense of shape that few designers ever achieve. She's quite a boat for her size. Four can sleep in reasonable comfort, there are six feet of headroom under the trunk cabin, and on deck there's enough space between the mast and the cabin to carry a dinghy. Yet she's a good sailer—far better, according to some, than she has a right to be—considering all the room she has down inside and on deck. *Annie* is a new boat from this old design and it would be hard to find a better job of boatbuilding.

Annie was the hit of the 1981 Wooden Boat Show in Newport and always has admirers wherever she sails.

LOA: 24'0"   Beam: 8'8"
Designed by Fenwick C. Williams
Built 1980 by Arundel Shipyard, Kennebunkport, Maine
Photographed at Kennebunkport

FREDA

A sloop into her second century

The many curves in a boat's cabin make it very different from a room in a house—and, for my money, a far more interesting place to be. *Freda*'s cabin has more curves than we consider normal these days. True to its age, the cabin's front is steam-bent round, and its top is highly crowned. Cast bronze opening ports are used rather than windows, and, even though they're small, a skylight and white paint compensate to make the cabin light and cheery.

Freda is pure Victorian: vertical tongue-and-groove staving for bulkheads and doors, an abundance of ornate trim moldings, a pair of fancy hanging knees. The built-in commode to starboard, opposite the enclosed toilet room, also harks back to an earlier time. Yes, *Freda* is a charmer, and, with clipper bow and gaff rig, as distinctive above deck as she is below.

LOA: 33'0"   Beam: 12'2"
Modeled and built 1885 by Harry Cookson,
   Belvedere, California
Photographed in San Francisco Bay

NORTHERN CROWN

A cutter with Danish roots

Although K. Aage Nielsen, *Northern Crown's* designer, left his native Denmark at an early age to join John G. Alden's Boston-based yacht design office, boats like this indicate that he never completely abandoned his heritage. The beautifully sculpted hull terminating in a distinctly Danish double-ended stern—combined with a contemporary American underwater profile and tall cutter rig—represents an incredibly successful marriage of diverse traditions and makes this 35-footer one of Nielsen's finest design concepts. There were 18-footers, 26-footers, and a 42-footer—all variations on the same theme and all built in Denmark. The 42-footer, embodied in the ketch-rigged *Holger Danske*, took top honors in the Bermuda Race a few years back.

In the lower right-hand picture, *Northern Crown* is herself after top honors in a recent race. She's a robust boat with lots of beam and displacement, but a powerful one—and she's known to be very slippery.

LOA: 35'6"   Beam: 11'5"
Designed by K. Aage Nielsen
Built 1956 by A. Walsted Baadevaerft, Thurø, Denmark
Photographed in Eggemoggin Reach, Maine

AIDA

A cruising yawl with 3' draft

What makes a boat's interior a good place to be? A combination of elements: a place to sit, cook, sleep, and otherwise function comfortably; a variety of shapes and textures to make it interesting; the simplicity and symmetry to make it restful. In short, a successful interior should be a treat to the eye as well as the body. There are some key factors at work to produce that effect here in the Herreshoff yawl *Aida*: a symmetrically arranged main cabin that can be shut off from the galley; an opening skylight over the cabin table; raised-panel bulkheads and doors; exquisitely proportioned structural members that are visually harmonious; a pair of exceptionally comfortable, 6½-foot-long settee-berths separated by a centerboard-trunk-mounted, drop-leaf table (a setup that always seems to encourage good conversation). Off-white paint, with a little naturally finished mahogany, gives this lovely cabin its finishing touch.

LOA: 33'6"   Beam: 9'2"
Designed by N.G. Herreshoff
Built 1926 by the Herreshoff Mfg. Co., Bristol,
    Rhode Island
Photographed in Eggemoggin Reach, Maine

FREE SPIRIT

A Concordia 33 sloop

Since the 1930s, more and more summertime sailors have found family yachting as embodied in a comfortable, modest, four-berth auxiliary cruiser more to their liking—and more to their pocketbooks—than the long-ended, deep-keeled, and generally cramped racing craft of earlier decades. The design for this Concordia 33-footer came out of that era. In more recent times, the trend toward practicality has been carried to its limits and perhaps beyond, by putting the accommodations for four into an ever-smaller hull—so that today a new boat the size of *Free Spirit* would probably be crowded with berths for six people.

Free Spirit is a sloop with a double-headsail rig, meaning that there are two jib-type sails ahead of the mast: a staysail fitted with a club at its foot so as to be self-tending when the boat tacks, and a roller-furling genoa running from the end of the bowsprit to the head of the mast. There's a lot of drive in the big genoa when unrolled and sheeted home, and it's truly a wonderful sail for light and moderate winds. When it breezes up, however, it's an easy matter to roll up the genoa (it can be done from the cockpit) and to use only the staysail. Such an easily reduced rig is a great convenience for cruising, a time when one is likely to be short-handed.

For some years, *Free Spirit* has been home-ported on the Maine coast. As one of the world's best cruising grounds, it's an ideal place for a boat like her. The combination of this boat and this place must be good for her owner, too: in being part of scenes like these, one's own spirit becomes decidedly free.

LOA: 33'5"   Beam: 9'9"
Designed by the Concordia Co.
Built 1948 by R. Ferguson, New Bedford, Massachusetts
Photographed off Brooklin, Maine

ROGUE

A yawl based on the Herreshoff Newport 29

About 30 years ago, with a change in rating rules, yawl rigs went out of style as racing boats. But the yawl rig will always have some distinct advantages for cruising boats such as *Rogue*. The mizzen, small and easily handled, is stepped on the afterdeck out of the way. If sheeted in, it will weathercock the boat and hold her head-to-wind, a real blessing if you're short-handed and trying to anchor or get underway without power. Because a yawl's mizzen is so far aft, even a small one has great influence on the boat's steering. Trimmed in or slacked off, set or furled, the mizzen can be used to balance a boat so she'll steer better. For the same reason, the mizzen is an effective heavy-weather sail when combined with only a storm jib.

There's not quite enough wind yet for *Rogue* to shorten sail, but when the time comes, it can be a matter of just dropping the mainsail. What could be simpler?

LOA: 36'9"   Beam: 10'6"
Designed by N.G. Herreshoff
Built 1953 by Seth Persson, Old Saybrook, Connecticut
Photographed off Nassau, Bahamas

TORNA

A Maine Coast class yawl

A springtime launching is a call for celebration—even if the boat is not new and, like *Torna*, has seen many a springtime come and go. Spring is generally when the annual painting and outfitting is completed and the boat looks her best; and, more often than not, launching day is a beauty. It's usually a weekday before vacations have started, so the owner rarely shows up—sadly, to his loss. Nor, with their busy schedule, do the boatyard workers have time to enjoy the fruits of their labor. Here's one launching, however, that we can celebrate vicariously, because the camera caught *Torna* only moments before she slid down the railway.

Torna and two other Maine Coast class yawls were designed and built on the heels of World War II, and over the years they've demonstrated that fine boats tend to attract appreciative owners. Through consistent care and understanding, all three remain in good condition even though they're now close to 50 years old.

LOA: 37'0"   Beam: 9'8"
Designed by E. Farnham Butler
Built 1947 by Mt. Desert Yacht Yard, Mt. Desert, Maine
Photographed at Seal Cove Boatyard, Brooksville, Maine

MARY ANN

A Barnegat Bay A-cat

Far from her native New Jersey, and fresh out of the Brooklin, Maine, shop of Benjamin River Marine, where she was given a brand-new hull, the 1922 Barnegat Bay A-cat *Mary Ann* is shown here undergoing sailing trials. Unlike most traditional, gaff-rigged catboats, A-cats were rigged marconi-style and given hollow masts nearly 50' long, as well as the more complex rigging needed to keep them standing. A-cats are shallow, unballasted center-boarders that depend upon their hull shape (broad beam and flaring topsides) and live weight (crew members laid out along the windward rail, when necessary) for stability. In windy weather, these boats have to be sailed with the greatest respect.

Mary Ann was the first boat of the class, and her great speed caused a bit of a sensation when she first appeared. Remarkably, three other original 1920s-vintage A-cats (along with a couple of other recently-built ones) still compete for the Toms River Challenge Cup, said to be the country's oldest continuously raced-for yachting trophy.

LOA: 28'2"   Beam: 10'10"
Designed by Charles D. Mower
Built 1922 by Morton Johnson & Co., Bay Head,
    New Jersey; new hull 1988 by Benjamin River Marine,
    Brooklin, Maine
Photographed in Brooklin

CIRCE

An Alden Triangle class sloop

In the nearly 70 years of her life, *Circe* has given her owners a lot of fun for their money. She's basically a daysailer, originally designed for racing in Massachusetts Bay with a fleet of identical boats. Later, when the class became "obsolete," *Circe* and her sisters were sold off individually and could be found all up and down the New England coast, put to a variety of uses and loved for a variety of reasons. They are simple boats, yet they are fast, safe, and beautiful to look at. They'll give you a thrilling sail no matter what the wind, without the bother and expense of a whole lot of light-weather sails. Their cockpits are big enough to hold a half-dozen people and they'll spin on a dime; their small cabins even allow cruising—as long as comfort isn't too high on your list of priorities. Triangles and other knockabout types, even though no longer in vogue, are well-built and continue to be among the best buys on the used-boat market.

Consider for a moment what it's like to sail a boat like this, with a big mainsail and a small, club-footed jib. After the sails are up, you sit at the tiller and steer, adjusting the sheets occasionally for whatever your point of sailing. *Circe* handles like a dream compared to most contemporary 28' sailboats with their handkerchief-sized mainsails and big, low-cut, unwieldy headsails. Judged by square feet of sail area alone, the newer rigs are fast. But there's more to sailing than aerodynamic efficiency: what about being able to tack instantly simply by moving the tiller, for example? (*Circe*'s jib is self-tending.) And how about the cost savings and convenience of a rig that goes fast in light weather—even downwind—without extra sails? Or what about being able to see to leeward because there's no vision-blocking genoa?

LOA: 28'5"   Beam: 7'6"
Designed by John G. Alden
Built 1925 by Graves Yacht Yard, Marblehead,
  Massachusetts
Photographed in Eggemoggin Reach, Maine

ELFITZ

A Winter Harbor 21 class knockabout

Beginning in 1907 as a seven-boat fleet and becoming nine boats strong by 1924, these gaff-rigged knockabouts were the yacht club's dominant racing class in Winter Harbor, Maine. In the 1950s, after half a century of use, apathy took hold and the fleet scattered—sold at low prices to the first buyers who came along. Only *Elfitz* and one other boat remained, although they were seldom used, through a two-decade hiatus. Because of their unusually fine design and construction, the other boats survived as well, even though some were neglected, abused, and altered. Thanks to a vibrant new interest in the Winter Harbor 21s, all nine boats are back where they started, fully restored and each with a different color scheme. Under the ownership of club members, these knockabouts compete against each other twice a week "as usual." Some have even been purchased by the original families, to be sailed by the grandchildren and great-grandchildren.

LOA: 31'6"   Beam: 7'3"
Designed by A.H. Packard (of Burgess & Packard)
Built 1924 by Geo. F. Lawley & Son, Neponset,
  Massachusetts
Photographed at Winter Harbor, Maine

EAGLET

and other Dark Harbor 20s

Sailboat racing has been an afternoon pastime in Islesboro, Maine, since the summer residents built their grand cottages there nearly a century ago. Since 1935, the chosen boats have been Dark Harbor 20s, a class of marconi-rigged sloops specially designed and built for the purpose. Before then, there were Dark Harbor 12s and 17s—gaff-riggers that stayed in vogue for some three decades.

Why does a single design (and the individual boats built to it) hang on for so long in Islesboro while a variety of boats come and go in most other places? There are several reasons. Since there's no interclub racing, the designs used by other yacht clubs aren't an influence. Also, the people here tend not to chase the latest fad in anything, including boats. The season is short—the Fourth of July to Labor Day—and for the rest of the year, as the picture at left shows, the boats are stored in sheds that protect them from the weather. Most of the Dark Harbor 20s are still in beautiful condition, after more than half a century—ready, perhaps, to remain the boat of choice for the next 50 years.

LOA: 30'2"   Beam: 6'9"
Designed by Sparkman & Stephens, Inc.
Built 1935 by Geo. F. Lawley & Son, Neponset,
  Massachusetts
Photographed at Islesboro, Maine

YACHTS OF FRIESLAND

Here at de Veenhoop, a small settlement in the Dutch province of Friesland, is a two-day, end-of-the-season gathering of traditional sailing craft. We attended the rendezvous as guests of Pier and Maria Piersma and Sicco and Ellen van Albada and cruised with them on inland canals aboard *Phoenix* and *De Lytse Bear* (lower right), a *boeier* and a *Staverse jol*, respectively, with the tjotter *Froask* (upper right) in tow. At de Veenhoop, the *aken*, *bollen*, *grundels*, and *schouwen*, as well as the *boeiers*, *Friese jachten*, *jollen*, *tjotters*, and others of the more than two dozen recognized national types, all raced several times around a short course, where viewing each other's boats under sail seemed as important as winning the race. Almost all have leeboards and masts that pivot on tabernacles, and many have oak decks and hulls, varnished like those shown here; all are exceptionally lovely. These traditional sloops have been built in Friesland since about 1870, and replica building is still carried on. Appreciation for these craft is growing; 1,400 or so originals and replicas have been registered with a national maritime historical association that has established criteria to ensure that the boats within that association remain pure.

Photographed at de Veenhoop, Friesland, Netherlands

VINTAGE

A V-bottom scow schooner

Vintage makes a charming and wonderful coastal cruiser that, with her salty, traditional look, is appreciated wherever she goes. She's a scow schooner, a gaff-rigged sailing vessel whose shallow-draft hull has a transom at both ends. As is apparent in the photo at left, her blunt bow pushes a big wave ahead of it, and the hull's boxy shape could not be called seakindly. Yet there are mitigating advantages—such as an exceptional expanse on deck and considerable usable space below for accommodations and storage, and a hull structure that is simpler and cheaper to build than most. *Vintage* also has a shallow draft (she draws only 3' with the centerboard up) for exploring waters where deeper cruisers can't go.

To look her best, a vessel like *Vintage* has to be painted these time-honored traditional workboat colors; gloss white, varnish, or some other yachtlike treatment simply would not be "right."

LOA: 45'0"   Beam: 15'0"
Designed by Capt. R.D. Culler
Built 1986 by Brooklin Boat Yard, Brooklin, Maine
Photographed at Brooklin

ELLEN

A traditional pinky schooner

For a boat that pulls on the heartstrings, the New England pinky schooner rates high. Pinkies were among our earliest offshore fishing craft. While anchored hundreds of miles at sea on the shallow tide-ridden, notoriously rough fishing banks, their crews used simple handlines over the rail—summer and winter—without benefit of engine, radio, or electronic aids to navigation. As full-bodied double-enders with short rigs, pinkies rode the waves like gulls. Although not noted for their speed to wind-ward, they could survive at sea, in comfort, during the worst of conditions.

Ed Porter, experienced in schooners and a longtime admirer of the pinky, wanted to see what one would be like for family cruising. Going the traditional route, he had one built without an engine or electrical system, and he fitted her out with cotton sails and natural-fiber rigging. Each year, *Ellen* makes the passage across the Bay of Fundy from Nova Scotia to cruise the Maine coast. Sailing aboard *Ellen* with the Porters is a most pleasant adventure; although you're somewhat subject to the whim of the wind, you're prepared to take whatever weather might come along.

LOA: 36'0"   Beam: 11'6"
Designed by Edward Porter based on plans published
*   by H.I. Chapelle*
Built 1981 by Stephen Slauenwhite, Mader's Cove,
*   Nova Scotia, Canada*
Photographed on Eggemoggin Reach, Maine

CONJURER

A Cape Cod catboat

*C*onjurer is a pure Cape Cod catboat, the real thing: barn-door rudder; oval coaming; a beam that's about half her length; a single, unstayed, solid mast up forward; shallow draft; and a huge wooden centerboard. For their length, catboats are tremendously roomy, at least in a horizontal sense—there's no way to get full headroom in such a shallow hull fitted with only a low trunk cabin. These boats carry plenty of sail, making them slip along even when there's only a little wind. A traditional gaff rig is the natural partner of the wide catboat hull, and that combination, in the hands of a good catboat sailor, can maneuver against the lightest of zephyrs, as is being done here. Notice at left that the mainsheet is slacked away for maximum boat speed. Over-trimming would jeopardize steerageway as well as risk missing this important, about-to-be-executed tack.

LOA: 27'6"   Beam: 12'6"
Modeled and built 1909 by H. Manley Crosby,
    Osterville, Massachusetts
Photographed at Center Harbor, Brooklin, Maine

AMITY

An original Friendship sloop

Amity is a genuine turn-of-the-century Friendship sloop, one of the 400 or so crafted by Wilbur Morse for local fishermen when these were the boats of choice up and down Maine's Mid-coast. But *Amity's* commercial career ended long ago during a wholesale shift to power-driven lobsterboats, and she, like many of her sisters, was made over into a pleasure craft. Since then, attrition has dwindled even the converted Friendships, and today *Amity*, although considerably rebuilt, is one of the few survivors.

Forming such beautiful craft from oak and pine and iron took time and talent and, above all, an enlightened sense of aesthetics. As the arts flourished in post-Civil War America, even workboat builders were swept up in a passion for sweet line and charming character, stimulated by what they saw going on around them. Nowadays, cost-effectiveness and efficiency govern commercial boat design, leading to a scarcity of beautiful boats like *Amity*, with their elliptical sterns and clipper bows.

LOA: 30'3"   Beam: 10'0"
Modeled and built 1901 by Wilbur A. Morse,
   Friendship, Maine
Photographed in the Benjamin River, Brooklin, Maine

WILLIAM M. RAND

A recently-built Friendship sloop

As a type, the Friendship sloop has held its charm far longer than it held onto its originally conceived utility. So popular has this traditional design remained, that for the past three decades there have been formal get-togethers each summer under the auspices of the Friendship Sloop Society, which also maintains a register of extant Friendships—the replicas as well as the originals. No matter when built, a Friendship has a salty look that appeals to many and is irresistible to those who are inspired to own one. Wooden-hulled Friendships built nowadays, such as the *William M. Rand*, are for pleasure instead of fishing, and they're generally put together of better materials and with more care than were the originals. Back then workboats were quickly turned out "for a price," often of green wood with iron fastenings.

LOA: 22'4"   Beam: 7'4"
Designed by McKie W. Roth
Built 1982 by John B. Rand, Lincoln, Massachusetts
Photographed in Penobscot Bay, Maine

CHAPTER II

POWERBOATS

For speed and convenience in waterborne transportation, many would argue that powerboats are the only way to go. And a growing number of aficionados contend that powerboating is best enjoyed in classics built of wood. Surprisingly, many of today's classic powerboats rolled out of the shops as stock units, as alike in appearance as Chevrolets. But like the roadsters and phaetons of the antique auto world, the sportier stockboats—mostly varnished mahogany runabouts—built by Chris-Craft, Gar Wood, and others, have always been coveted. Just ask Jenny Larter.

Jenny's Chris-Craft runabout, *Foxy Lady*, already carried this name when she got it, but she did manage to give her dog, Barnstormer Bear, an equally imaginative label. Jenny flies an open-cockpit Stearman "barnstormer" airplane whenever *Foxy Lady* feels too slow. Today the runabout suffices, however, as it virtually flies down New York's Lake George.

Among the 113 different models Chris-Craft offered as the depressed 1930s came to a close was this barrel-backed runabout for which the firm advertised speeds of 40 miles an hour. Chris-Craft claimed then to be the world's largest builder of motorboats. Indeed, these increasingly streamlined, mahogany-planked craft, ranging in size from 15½' to 55', came off assembly lines where precut pieces were all ready to be fastened together. It wasn't exactly like Detroit, but the plant was in Michigan and the United Auto Workers controlled its labor force. Chris-Craft founder Chris Smith, known as the Henry Ford of boatbuilding, went to his grave in 1939, the same year *Foxy Lady* was built.

FOXY LADY, *a Chris-Craft barrel-backed runabout* *LOA: 19'0"* *Beam: 6'0"* *Designed and built 1939 by Chris-Craft Corp., Algonac, Michigan* *Photographed on Lake George, New York*

AIDA II

A Fay & Bowen launch

Speed seems to have become the criterion for modern powerboat enjoyment. To be sure, going fast in a speedboat provides short-term thrills, with noise, flying spray, and a rough ride, but such thrills eventually become exhausting, and then even boring. Too bad that going slow doesn't enjoy equal status among manufacturers, advertisers, and consumers. As these photographs show, a good deal of pleasure can come from putt-putting along, leisurely, at four or five miles an hour.

Aida II was a standard offering of the Fay & Bowen Engine Company of Geneva, New York, whose production began in 1907. Designated a "family launch" and equipped with only 10 horsepower, *Aida ll* was never meant for speed. But she has other virtues, among them economy: her classic hull glides through the water so easily that a 10-dollar bill buys the gas for an entire season.

LOA: 25'11"   Beam: 5'6"
Designed and built about 1915 by Fay & Bowen Engine
    Co., Geneva, New York
Photographed on Lake Placid, New York

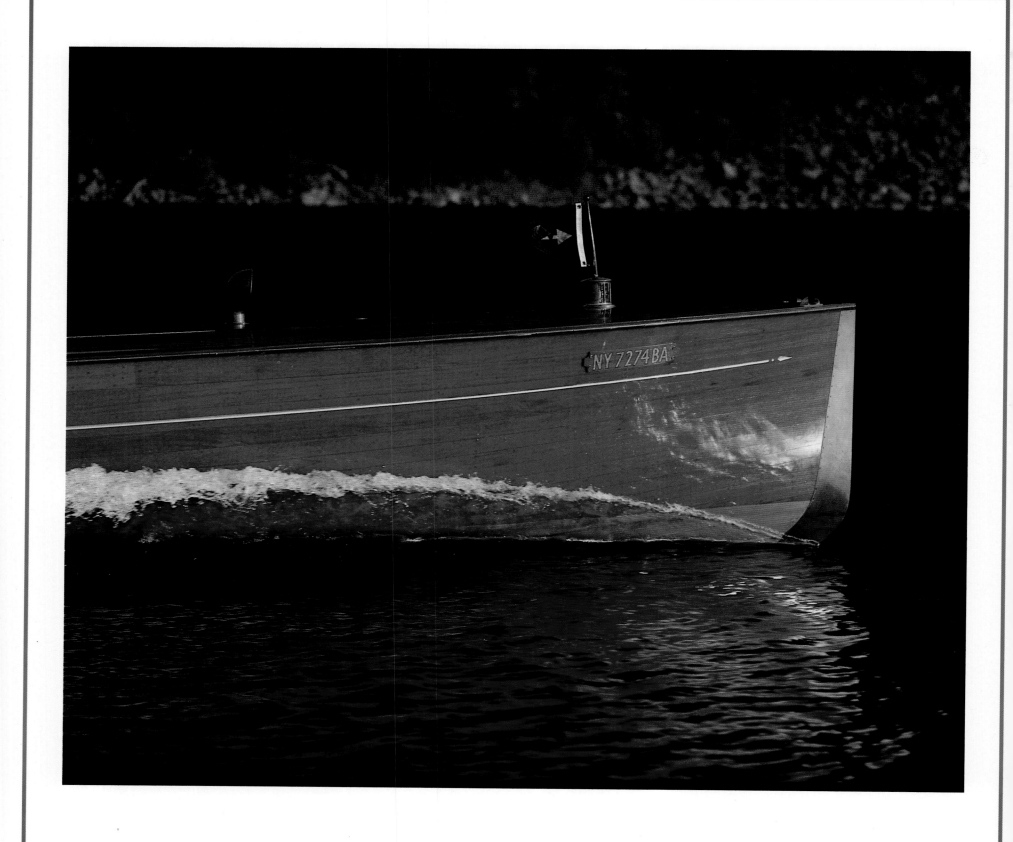

THE GOLDEN ARROW

A Fay & Bowen runabout

Varnished mahogany hulls with polished brass trim evoke all manner of compliments, especially when the reflection of low evening light produces this awesome a result. But on the heels of such words usually come comments about the great amount of work that must go into caring for boats like these. True, there is a lot of sanding, cleaning, brushing, and rubbing, but these tasks have their rewards— and there are techniques for doing them that somewhat reduce the time. But the environment can also play a major role. When not in use, *The Golden Arrow* hangs clear of the water in her own boathouse, where, sheltered from rain and shaded from sun, she requires little attention. And in her landlocked home waters of Lake George, New York, this classic runabout is free from the corrosive effects of salt air and seawater.

LOA: 30'0"   Beam: 6'4"
Designed by Morris M. Whitaker
Built 1924 by Fay & Bowen Engine Co.,
   Geneva, New York
Photographed on Lake George, New York

BABY BOOTLEGGER

An original Gold Cup winner

*B*aby Bootlegger, as one might guess from the name, is a product of the Roaring Twenties—with the speed and panache of a Duesenberg, the bobbed tail of an Auburn Speedster, and the smooth ride of a Packard touring car. Restored (in the purest sense of the word) from derelict condition to its original elegance, *Baby Bootlegger* is an ambassador from another era—from a time when boats performed, but did so with real style. The speed is a comfortable 60 miles an hour, and there's that rare, finely crafted elegance born of the marriage between a good design and superb construction. She belonged originally to millionaire sportsman Caleb Bragg, who twice drove her to victory in the Gold Cup Race, the most important of all speedboat events.

Her streamlined stern overhangs the aft end of her hull just clear of the water and provides a place to attach the rudder and propeller shaft bearing. The idea here was to get the propeller itself several feet aft of the waterborne part of the boat so it could run in less disturbed water. It worked and so did a lot of other features, due to the skill and experience of the designer, Professor George Crouch. Although less well remembered than John Hacker or Gar Wood, Crouch was a leading designer of planing hulls and was the first to come up with the concave V-shaped bottom that gives *Baby Bootlegger* her speed and smooth ride.

LOA: 29'10"   Beam: 5'11"
Designed by George F. Crouch
Built 1924 by Henry B. Nevins, Inc., City Island,
    New York
Photographed on Lake George, New York

MISS COLUMBIA

A replica of a Gold Cup racer

Working from the same George Crouch drawings that New York's Nevins yard used in building the original *Miss Columbia* in 1924, Mark Mason oversaw the construction of this replica 60-odd years later. Drawings, no matter how complete, don't always show every detail, but Mark was in the unique position of already owning another Crouch/Nevins Gold Cup racer, *Baby Bootlegger* (shown on the preceding page) with which he was intimately familiar. A more authentic job would be hard to imagine, or, with Bill Cooper building the hull and Harold Rivard restoring the engine, one having better workmanship. The Gold Cup spans more than 80 years and the variety of boats that have raced for it is infinite. By far the most practical Gold Cuppers are from the mid-1920s, when the racing rules outlawed hydroplanes, limited the engine displacement, and encouraged elegant, smooth-riding 50-mile-an-hour craft like *Miss Columbia*. It's little wonder this "gentleman's runabout" racing design was selected for replication.

LOA: 26′10″   Beam: 6′3″
Designed by George F. Crouch
Built 1986 under supervision of Mark Mason
Photographed on Lake Winnipesaukee,
*   New Hampshire*

VINTAGE MAHOGANY
SPEEDBOATS

 *1915 Hutchinson*
USA 41

 *1954 Chris-Craft*
USA 41

 *1939 Hacker-Craft*
USA 41

 *1931 Gar Wood*
USA 41

 *1954 Chris-Craft*
USA 41

 *1939 Hacker-Craft*
USA 41

 *1931 Gar Wood*
USA 41

 *1915 Hutchinson*
USA 41

 *1915 Hutchinson*
USA 41

 *1954 Chris-Craft*
USA 41

 *1939 Hacker-Craft*
USA 41

 *1931 Gar Wood*
USA 41

P1111

VINTAGE MAHOGANY

SPEEDBOATS

From the mid-1920s through the 1930s, American craftsmen raised the design and construction of wooden pleasure boats to an art form. Influenced by rapid advances in the look and performance of contemporary automobiles, boat manufacturers combined their passion for detail with sleek hulls, chrome hardware, and powerful engines. The result was an incomparably beautiful marriage of speed and grace.

The high-quality, low-cost crafts of this period made recreational boating attractive and widely affordable. With a promise of luxury, reliability, easy handling, and comfort, these stylish wooden boats became floating pieces of the American dream. They also brought the country together. Eager to share long, carefree days with friends and loved ones, more and more Americans took to the waters to enjoy the thrill of the race and the profits of relaxation.

The golden age of vintage mahogany speedboats lasted through the 1950s, when materials like fiberglass and aluminum changed the nature of American boatbuilding. Yet their unmatched charm continues to fire the imaginations of both novices and lifelong boating enthusiasts. Symbolic of a bygone era, elegant wooden boats remind us not only that fun can be simple and wholesome, but also that freedom is within our grasp.

Gar Wood 33-foot triple cockpit runabouts are considered some of the finest stock runabouts produced by the famous firm in Marysville, Michigan. Elegant and powerful, these crafts were offered with either a Scripps V-12 or a Gar Wood Liberty V-12 engine and were capable of speeds in excess of 50 miles per hour.

Based on the streamlined designs of John Hacker, *Thunderbird* is a 55-foot commuter boat featuring a distinctive stainless-steel cabin top. Built in 1939 by the Huskins Boat Company of Bay City, Michigan, its original 550-horsepower engines were replaced in the 1960s with twin 1000-horsepower Allison V-12 aircraft engines.

A steady seller since 1936, the Racing Runabout exemplified Chris-Craft speed and design through 1954. Updated after World War II, the 19-foot model features a split cockpit and gleaming deck hardware. With its 158-horsepower MBL engine, this craft can operate at 40 miles per hour or more.

A popular style for touring and commuting, the long-deck launch was powered by a 4-cylinder or 6-cylinder marine engine and could reach speeds close to 30 miles per hour. This attractive 30-foot craft was custom-built in 1915 by Hutchinson Brothers Boat Company in Alexandria Bay, New York.

A popular style for touring and commuting, the long-deck launch was powered by a 4-cylinder or 6-cylinder marine engine and could reach speeds close to 30 miles per hour. This attractive 30-foot craft was custom-built in 1915 by Hutchinson Brothers Boat Company in Alexandria Bay, New York.

Gar Wood 33-foot triple cockpit runabouts are considered some of the finest stock runabouts produced by the famous firm in Marysville, Michigan. Elegant and powerful, these crafts were offered with either a Scripps V-12 or a Gar Wood Liberty V-12 engine and were capable of speeds in excess of 50 miles per hour.

Based on the streamlined designs of John Hacker, *Thunderbird* is a 55-foot commuter boat featuring a distinctive stainless-steel cabin top. Built in 1939 by the Huskins Boat Company of Bay City, Michigan, its original 550-horsepower engines were replaced in the 1960s with twin 1000-horsepower Allison V-12 aircraft engines.

A steady seller since 1936, the Racing Runabout exemplified Chris-Craft speed and design through 1954. Updated after World War II, the 19-foot model features a split cockpit and gleaming deck hardware. With its 158-horsepower MBL engine, this craft can operate at 40 miles per hour or more.

Gar Wood 33-foot triple cockpit runabouts are considered some of the finest stock runabouts produced by the famous firm in Marysville, Michigan. Elegant and powerful, these crafts were offered with either a Scripps V-12 or a Gar Wood Liberty V-12 engine and were capable of speeds in excess of 50 miles per hour.

Based on the streamlined designs of John Hacker, *Thunderbird* is a 55-foot commuter boat featuring a distinctive stainless-steel cabin top. Built in 1939 by the Huskins Boat Company of Bay City, Michigan, its original 550-horsepower engines were replaced in the 1960s with twin 1000-horsepower Allison V-12 aircraft engines.

A steady seller since 1936, the Racing Runabout exemplified Chris-Craft speed and design through 1954. Updated after World War II, the 19-foot model features a split cockpit and gleaming deck hardware. With its 158-horsepower MBL engine, this craft can operate at 40 miles per hour or more.

A popular style for touring and commuting, the long-deck launch was powered by a 4-cylinder or 6-cylinder marine engine and could reach speeds close to 30 miles per hour. This attractive 30-foot craft was custom-built in 1915 by Hutchinson Brothers Boat Company in Alexandria Bay, New York.

x
$4.

UNITED STATES POSTAL SERVICE ®

© 2006 USPS

PLATE POSITION

461800

KIYI

A power cruiser from Puget Sound

Kiyi has a style rarely found in a craft as small as 50 feet. In fact, her proportions are so perfect she could pass, at quick glance, for a much larger classic power cruiser. She has style to spare, and has long been a favorite in Pacific Northwest waters. Actually, *Kiyi* is small for her length because of her narrow beam and low freeboard—designed back when beauty was more important and roominess less sought after. Even so, she makes a comfortable cruiser, with sleeping quarters under the foredeck and a galley, enclosed head, and main saloon in the aft cabin. The skipper has the option of steering either from the shelter of the pilothouse or from the open bridge ahead of the stack.

There's potential for cruising all year long in *Kiyi*'s home waters of Puget Sound, in spite of the sometimes damp and cool weather. When you're aboard *Kiyi*, lying in a quiet cove surrounded by spectacular scenery with the cabin stove warming both coffee and crew, the closed-in character of Northwest powerboats begins to make a great deal of sense.

LOA: 50'0"   *Beam: 10'4"*
Designed by Leigh Coolidge
Built 1926 by Schertzer Bros., Lake Union,
    Seattle, Washington
Photographed at Port Madison, Washington

MER-NA

A Blanchard dreamboat

In selecting a boat well suited for cruising the waters of Puget Sound, *Mer-Na* would come out a sure winner. The scenery there is so beautiful that you'd miss a lot by rushing past in a speedier, higher-powered boat. *Mer-Na*, as you can see, is mostly cabin, and she has a wood stove for the cheeriest kind of heat. The clear, 360-degree view from her enclosed pilothouse makes it a great place for enjoying what's around, even in inclement weather. A smooth-running, quiet gasoline engine is an especially good shipmate in this age of the rumbling diesel. The boat is rigged for easy anchoring and for taking her dinghy aboard. Mer-Na has been recognized as a winner in other ways as well: at the annual Victoria (British Columbia) Classic Boat Festival, she was named Best Powerboat Overall— top honors in a top event.

LOA: 36'0"   Beam: 9'0"
Designed by Leigh Coolidge
Built 1930 by N.J. Blanchard Boat Co.,
*   Seattle, Washington*
Photographed off Sidney, British Columbia, Canada

BIRCHES

An 11-passenger runabout by Chris-Craft

Although most varnished-mahogany runabouts were saltwater-compatible— built with nonferrous fastenings and hardware—the boats that have survived the longest are the ones such as *Birches*, kept on fresh water. She originated at the Chris-Craft factory in Algonac, Michigan, was delivered to Clayton, New York, and spent many years on Lake George, also in New York. Later she returned to Algonac for some restoration, then found herself on beautiful Lake Tahoe, for the final touches.

Birches still carries her original name and her original Chris-Craft 824-cubic-inch flathead V-8 engine (model A-120). This 28' custom runabout— one of 37 different models offered in 1931—was advertised with speeds up to 42 miles an hour for a price of $5,395, including her extra-high-quality "streamlined" hardware.

LOA: 28'0" Beam: 7'0"
Designed and built 1931 by Chris-Craft Corp.,
Algonac, Michigan
Photographed on Lake Tahoe

COMET

An aft-cabin launch

Comet is a kind of seagoing limousine, providing a fast ride in luxury with someone else doing the driving. Indeed, these speedboats of the 1920s had the same appeal as Auburn speedsters, Cords, and Duesenbergs: rare and expensive, noisy and fast, but above all beautiful classics that can turn as many heads and draw as many admiring comments at age 70 as when brand-new.

Lake Tahoe, where this picture was taken, is a Mecca for these splendid craft—and little wonder. Summer residents with enough money to support their passions are drawn here by the beauty of the scenery and the perfect climate. Travel between the lakeside homes is faster by speedboat than by auto. And people like Dick Clarke and his Sierra Boat Company provide expert restoration and care. Here is a spectacular fleet of top-of-the-line classic speedboats being well used and well cared for. It's historic preservation with a great deal of style!

LOA: 36'0"   Beam: 7'0"
Designed and built 1921 by Fellows & Stewart,
*   Wilmington, California*
Photographed on Lake Tahoe

THUNDERBIRD

The ultimate Hacker express cruiser

The roar of power, the flash of speed, the gleam of varnished wood, and the sparkle of polished metal—that's pleasure-boating on Lake Tahoe, where classic wooden launches, speedboats, and runabouts by the hundreds serve both practical and ornamental purposes.

Thunderbird, overqualified in most company, stands out even among the impressive Lake Tahoe fleet. Surely John Hacker had an airplane in mind when he designed her in 1939; she looks as though, given wings, she could easily fly. As a boat, there's nothing like her; as a monument to the heyday of prewar streamlining, *Thunderbird* stands supreme.

LOA: 55'0"   Beam: 11'10"
*Designed and built 1940 by John L. Hacker,
    Bay City, Michigan
Photographed on Lake Tahoe*

AN ALBURY RUNABOUT FROM MAN-O-WAR

Places like that shown on the facing page abound in the Bahamas, but they're on the small, off-lying islands and you have to get there on your own; you need a boat. With some luck, especially in Nassau or the Abacos, you might find one of these Albury-built outboard runabouts for hire. Built on Man-o-War Cay, they're put together and finished as nicely as any wooden boat you're likely to encounter. With moderately deep-Vee hulls and full-length spray rails, they're smooth-riding and dry. Framed with tough natural crooks of horseflesh and planked with Andros pine—both are island woods—these boats are very rugged. One livery in Nassau, in fact, refuses to deal in any other boat, claiming that these Albury runabouts will stand up to abuse better than any other type. Because these craft are built locally of native materials, they fit naturally into scenes like this and become an important part of the beautiful view. Who could ask more of a boat?

LOA: 19'6"   Beam: 7'0"
Modeled and built 1982 by Willard Albury,
*   Man-o-War Cay, Abaco, Bahamas*
Photographed in Abaco Sound, Bahamas

BLACK KNIGHT

A luxury motoryacht

Beautiful things look even more so in the golden glow of the day's last light. Often the camera sees this better than the eye and preserves for us those fleeting moments to be savored later.

Black Knight, anchored close to the steep, spruce-clad Bucks Harbor, Maine, shore at a sunset high tide, isn't an everyday occurrence. But then *Black Knight* isn't an everyday yacht, either. Maintained impeccably, she has often served as the committee boat for big-time racing, including the *America*'s Cup series and the annual New York Yacht Club cruise. She emerged as *Cassiar* from the East Boothbay, Maine, shop of Goudy & Stevens in the late 1960s on the heels of the schooner-yacht *America II*. It was a time when big, wooden yacht-building was virtually dead elsewhere in the country, yet these vessels were crafted to standards enviable in any age. The skills run deep in East Boothbay, however, and they were put to use, some 20 years later—this time in the Hodgdon yard—on a near-sister to *Black Knight*.

LOA: 82'7"   Beam: 19'9"
Designed by Eldredge-McInnis, Inc.
Built 1968 by Goudy & Stevens, East Boothbay, Maine
Photographed at Bucks Harbor, South Brooksville, Maine

PAGAN

An electric-powered canoe

Almost nowhere could an electric-powered canoe find more suitable waters than on the upper reaches of the River Thames in England. Here there is enough shelter so that appearance rather than seaworthiness can govern a boat's design. And here, far from city noise, quiet propulsion can be fully appreciated. A day's outing in *Pagan*, with a picnic along the way, would be an unusually fine experience.

Pagan reached her present splendid condition through the dedication of her new owners, who wanted a proper job, and through the skill of Henwood and Dean of Henley-on-Thames, the boatbuilders who did the actual work. Starting with a near-derelict, this team of patron and craftsman produced a restoration that fully measures up to the enduring legacy of the beautiful Thames.

LOA: 20'0"   Beam: 4'0"
Modeled and built about 1920 probably by Jonathan Bond, Maidenhead, Berkshire, England
Photographed on the Thames River near Henley, Oxfordshire, England

PETER FREEBODY'S BOATSHOP

At Hurley, Berkshire, England

Busy is the English boatshop of Peter Freebody where there usually are a dozen or more Thames River-type watercraft being refurbished—and at least that many men working on them. These are not simply slavish restorations, since Freebody—whose family of Thames watermen can be traced back to the 13th century—has a true understanding of the boats and is perfectly capable of creating historically accurate interpretations. As the boats go into his shop, they are apt to be in dismal condition, such as the one in the right foreground of the facing page, whereas the finished boats feature beveled glass, gleaming new mahogany, polished brass, relief carvings, gold leaf, and sturdy rebuilt hulls. The 40' Edwardian saloon launch *Dorothy*, shown at left, is an example. Dating back to 1919, she's been elegantly restored, complete with a 1916 Buick engine, and is ready, once more, to resume her task of carrying passengers in stately elegance up and down this most historic of rivers.

KITTIWAKE

A Lake Windermere steam launch

If you're ever offered a ride on a steamboat, by all means accept. First you'll notice the quiet, and then the lack of vibration. In the words of George Pattinson, "It's a most civilized form of transport." Pattinson lives in England's Lake District—specifically, on Lake Windermere. In fact, to some, he is Mr. Windermere. Here he's shown at the controls of *Kittiwake*, one of nine old steam launches belonging to the Windermere Steamboat Museum, a built-out-over-the-water complex started by Pattinson in 1977 where turn-of-the-century-boats still operate, where you can buy a scheduled ride on one of them (and be served hot tea from a famed Windermere steam teakettle), and where a few gasoline-powered boats, sailing craft, and rowboats round out the collection. The Windermere watercraft, given shelter and reasonable care, have demonstrated how durable a wooden boat can be in a freshwater environment.

LOA: 40'0"   Beam: 7'0"
Modeled and built 1898 by T.W. Hayton, Windermere,
    Cumbria, England
Photographed on Lake Windermere

CHAPTER III

WORKING BOATS

These are the boats that earn or, in times past, have earned their keep from what they do. Practically speaking, they could be considered nothing more than tools for making money. But I'm pleased to report that the owners of the special boats shown here don't think that way—far from it, in fact. Because they are built of wood and have beauty of form and function measured on any scale, and because, luckily, they have attracted owners who appreciate those virtues, those owners take great pains to maintain them. There are two distinct types of working boats represented: those whose appearance and appeal attract business, as in the case of the passenger-carrying schooners of Maine, and the others, such as fishing boats, where function alone brings success. The first tend to shine with fresh paint and varnish, while the second may show the patina of wear. I think both types are heroic, especially so the ones that are worked the hardest and show where chafe and wear have taken their toll. Several of these (such as *Nellie*, shown here, and *Rosie Parks*, overleaf) have been retired and preserved.

The waterways no longer teem as they once did with commercial craft. Current economics and technology have diminished the need for the wonderfully diverse boats of the past built of natural and native materials. There are exceptions, however. Presented here are some of the survivors I hope have or will become precious enough with the passage of time to remain with us for years to come.

We begin with *Nellie*. One hundred years ago, when she was new, *Nellie* and her many sloop-rigged sisters harvested oysters along the Connecticut, New York, and New Jersey shorelines. Practical gasoline engines hadn't yet made their appearance, so power to drag three or four iron dredges came from sails or, when it served, from the swift current as it carried the boat over the oyster beds. Early "winders," powered by hand, hoisted each dredge aboard as it became full. Lining the shores, local buyers worked from floating oyster houses or ones built atop piers where oyster sloops would tie up and unload.

Today, we live in a faster-paced, increasingly synthetic world where such old-time scenes are becoming rare and remote. Fortunately, however, for both peace of mind and a sense of our own heritage, museums such as Mystic Seaport (where *Nellie*'s photograph was taken) serve us well. There, the past is very much present.

NELLIE, a Long Island Sound oyster sloop   *LOA: 32'7"   Beam: 12'5"   Modeled and built 1891 in Smithtown, New York   Photographed at Mystic Seaport Museum, Mystic, Connecticut*

JOYCE MARIE

A round-stern sardine carrier

The Maine sardine carriers have a pretty good life along the coast, at least for commercial craft. And, as a result, they've lasted well. *Joyce Marie*, for example, was built in 1948. These are inshore craft generally operating in sheltered waters; they're laid-up in the winter, and when in use their gear is light enough so there's little risk of damaging the boat. Their business is to take the small herring, or sardines, that run in schools along the coast in summer from the weirs and seines in which they've been trapped and deliver them to the canning factories. Sardine carriers, even in the days of sail, have never been burdensome craft and in fact have consistently been long, lean, and exceptionally graceful. Although in the underway photo *Joyce Marie* is loaded, she still slides along with comparatively little wake or disturbance.

Sardine carriers are factory-owned boats. It's been nearly 40 years since a new one has been built, and most of those now in use date from around the time of World War II. Newbert & Wallace built several others from the same model used for *Joyce Marie*, some of her length and some about 10 feet longer. They're beautiful boats in anyone's judgment and are admired wherever they go.

LOA: 73'0"   Beam: 18'0"
Modeled by Roy Wallace
Built 1948 by Newbert & Wallace, Thomaston, Maine
Photographed in Eggemoggin Reach and Southwest
    Harbor, Maine

MAINE LOBSTERBOATS

Spurred on by the production of newer and better engines, the Maine lobsterboat emerged from a four- or five-decade evolution as a beautiful and unusually efficient craft. The pilothouse provides shelter and contains the steering station, and there's a level and relatively unobstructed platform in the cockpit. The boat's bow is high and flares outward for driving into a sea without taking on too much solid water or spray. Farther aft, low freeboard eases the task of hoisting the traps aboard. If you think *Red Top II* looks as much at home on the water as a seagull, you're quite right. The Maine lobsterboat, like the gull, is about as perfect a blend of form and function as you're likely to see: maneuverable, seaworthy, and fast, besides being efficient and good-looking.

A Maine lobsterboat frequently stays overboard year round, even though it may see little use in the dead of winter. When the weather finally breaks, bottom painting can take place at low tide, as shown here with *Rainbow* and *Chris Dana*. Even when their boats are stored ashore, lobstermen always take care to launch well before the bottom planking's caulked seams start to open up. They are fully aware of the damage that can result from too much time out of the water.

RAINBOW
LOA: 36'10"   Beam: 11'8"
Modeled and built 1970 by Frank Osgood,
   Vinalhaven, Maine
Photographed at Vinalhaven

RED TOP II
LOA: 34'0"   Beam: 10'6"
Modeled and built 1968 by Harold Gower,
   Beals Island, Maine
Photographed off Isle au Haut, Maine

CHRIS DANA
LOA: 32'0"   Beam: 10'0"
Modeled and built 1952 by Makinen Bros.,
   South Thomaston, Maine
Photographed at Stonington, Maine

NOVA SCOTIA BOATS

Robust would be a good word to describe the working boats of Grand Manan, New Brunswick. These are big boats for their length—wide and deep and high. They're named for where they're built— the Canadian province of Nova Scotia—and they're as distinctive as tugboats. They are built differently from most powerboats as well, in that their softwood frames (usually hackmatack) act more as battens holding the planking together than as structural members giving the hull its shape. Hull shape as well as stiffness comes primarily from the bulkheads and floor timber assemblies, not from the frames themselves. By no means should these boats be thought of as weak, however; the unique construction has proven itself well able to withstand heavy use in the harsh Bay of Fundy working environment.

It was mid-November, the start of Grand Manan lobster season when these photos were taken. Most boats, and there are more than 100 of them fishing from this island, are wooden. On opening day, every boat sets its legal limit of 375 traps. Promptly at 8:00 A.M., each boat will race to where its skipper feels is the best lobstering bottom, drop its traps one by one, and race back like *Pat & Robbie* for another load. By day's end, some 55,000 traps will have been set, and the waters will be so thick with buoys that it's a case of setting the last of the traps wherever there is still room.

PAT & ROBBIE
LOA: 45'0"   Beam: 14'0'
Modeled by Roy Doucette
Built 1981 by Paul Doucette, Cape St. Mary,
*   Nova Scotia, Canada*

BRE-JO-CO
LOA: 38'0"   Beam: 13'0"
Modeled and built 1976 by Roy Doucette, Cape St. Mary,
*   Nova Scotia, Canada*

GERI II

A West Coast gill-netter

Geri II, a gill-netter working out of Anacortes, Washington, has benefited greatly from the long-time, caring ownership of Pete Padovan. *Geri II* is a one-man boat, and, like a well-groomed hunting dog, she's ready to begin her quest at a moment's notice. Recorded reports of openings and closings of the fishing grounds come over the telephone, and when Pete learns there's fishing in nearby waters, he and his boat are off. They'll fish until they're loaded or until the place is closed to them—these days, more often the latter. Nights aboard are common, and *Geri II* has a bunk and Spartan galley forward.

The 1,800-foot-long gill net rolls up on the big drum, guided during setting and hauling back by the stern-mounted rollers. While fishing, Pete operates the boat from a second steering station aft of the drum where he can see what's going on and pick off the salmon as the net brings them aboard.

LOA: 33'0"   Beam: 8'6"
Modeled and built 1955 in Steveston, British Columbia, Canada
Photographed off Anacortes, Washington

Keel Boats and Cobles of England's Yorkshire Coast

England's great tidal range affects all its boats and boating activities, and the watermen in the north-eastern part of the country also have to contend with long, shelving beaches and a scarcity of deep-water harbors. The boats there are hauled out directly after landing in the surf or, as in this Yorkshire town of Staithes, moored in a creek, where they ground out at low tide.

Boats that have to get out and in through heavy surf or take to the ground twice a day while moored need special characteristics: for example, a spade-like rudder that can easily be lifted off its hangers. Boats that work off a beach also need a pointed end that can be headed into the surf and held that way. The craft shown at left are mostly so-called double-ended keel boats used for day trips to the nearby fishing grounds. The red-hulled boat at right is a coble. They come and go as the tides serve and are individually tied off with a line from each quarter. In today's world of increasing complexity and "factory" fishing fleets, it's refreshing to know that simple shore-fishing boats like these can still make a living for their owners.

Modeled and built by various local builders
Photographed at Staithes, Yorkshire, England

CHARLES W. MORGAN

A New Bedford whaleship

The idea of a run-of-the-mill wooden whaleship lasting for more than 150 years would probably have astonished Jethro and Zachariah Hillman, the brothers whose New Bedford shipyard built the *Charles W. Morgan* in 1841. But the thought of her lasting another century and a half—and more besides—is generally accepted today because of the restoration and care she is being given by Mystic Seaport Museum, where she's a prized possession. The restoration, now complete (this photo is from 1983), resulted in nearly all new wood from the waterline up, a once-common repair technique for aging ships called retopping; but the lower half of her hull, which has been underwater and sheltered from the weather, is essentially the same one she was built with. Its condition is still good for many years yet.

There's a lot of bend in those new 3"- and 4"-thick planks at the bow and because it's limber, particularly when steamed, white oak is used here (left photo) and at the stern as well where there is considerable twist to the planking. Amidships, where the planks run straighter, longer pieces of the very durable heart pine (longleaf yellow pine heartwood) work best. Visitors find live exhibits of planking, framing, and decking-work to be fascinating, and in this museum they are encouraged to watch the process while it is explained to them.

LOA: 114'0"   Beam: 27'8"
Modeled and built 1841 by Hillman Bros.,
*   New Bedford, Massachusetts*
Photographed at Mystic Seaport Museum,
*   Mystic, Connecticut*

SUSAN H.

A tugboat from Puget Sound

A harbor tug, such as *Susan H.*, has to start, stop, reverse, and turn almost continuously as part of her daily routine. Tugboats are designed both for maneuverability and towing power, and that always demands a big, slow-turning propeller that gets a good "bite" on the water no matter what. Tugboat hulls have to be strong and deep enough aft to swing that huge propeller, and there has to be space enough inside for the engine, its big reduction gear, and considerable fuel. The size of her wake is a good indication that a lot of this tug's heavy-timbered wooden hull lies below the waterline.

The business end of any tug is her afterdeck, the location of her towing bitts and winches. In order to steer while towing, her bitts have to be forward of her rudder and the area astern of them kept clear for the swing of the towing cable. From high in the pilothouse, the captain can see nearly everything around him; when working close in, however, he can use the alternate controls next to the towing machinery aft.

Registered length: 55'4"   Beam: 16'0"
Built 1947 by Frank Prothero, Lake Union,
*   Seattle, Washington*
Photographed at Port Madison, Washington

TUG'N'GRUNT

A schooner's yawlboat

A yawlboat is like a little undecked tugboat fitted with lifting eyes at each end so it can be hoisted on the davits of its mother vessel. Like tugs, yawlboats swing a big propeller and have a big engine and reduction gear to match. Although their overall length is limited to only a little more than the distance between the big vessel's stern davits (yawlboats usually are between 14' and 17' long), they must be capable of pushing (or on occasion pulling) a vessel weighing from 50 to 200 tons. *Tug'n'Grunt*, then, is an appropriate name for this little workhorse. She was built to service the century-old 65' cruise schooner *Isaac H. Evans*, which sails the Maine coast each summer with paying passengers. Besides acting as the schooner's auxiliary engine when the wind fails or when maneuvering in close quarters is required, *Tug'n'Grunt* provides transportation from ship to shore or can be used as a waterborne work platform.

LOA: 14'6"   Beam: 5'10"
Designed and built 1979 by Capt. Douglas Lee,
*   North End Shipyard, Rockland, Maine*
Photographed in Mid-coast Maine

HERITAGE

A passenger-carrying coasting schooner

Tradition runs strong in the Maine schooner fleet, and the schooner *Heritage* reflects that tradition in more than name alone. Her hull is oak and pine, her sails are cotton canvas, her running rigging is natural-fiber manila, and when the wind dies she depends upon her deceptively small yawlboat to push her along. *Heritage* was designed and built between 1979 and 1983 by her owner-skipper, who based her on turn-of-the-century coasting schooners—the tractor-trailer trucks of their day—that carried goods from port to port up and down the Atlantic coast. These days, the cargoes for *Heritage* and the dozen or so other traditional schooners in the fleet are a different sort: hardy vacationers who sail the coast hoping to create their own links with the past.

When the wind rises and the water gets choppy and the yawlboat is no longer needed, she's hauled out on *Heritage*'s stern davits. This innocent-looking little powerhouse, appropriately named *Clark Kent*, may be small, but she's often called upon to be a Superboat—much like Superman's meek-looking alter ego.

LOA: 93'0"   Beam: 24'0"
Designed by Capt. Douglas Lee
Built 1983 by Capts. Doug and Linda Lee and Capt.
* John Foss, North End Shipyard, Rockland, Maine*
Photographed in Mid-coast Maine

MERCANTILE, LEWIS R. FRENCH, MARY DAY

Penobscot Bay schooners at Brooklin, Maine

Carrying passengers commercially in otherwise obsolete coasting schooners began before World War II when Captain Frank Swift bought the *Mercantile* (under sail at far left) and several other vessels, added Spartan accommodations, and started offering weeklong summertime cruises along the Maine coast. Swift's idea proved sound and as time passed, new schooners (such as the *Mary Day*) were built and others (such as the *Lewis R. French*) were restored to sail once again. Now the Penobscot Bay windjammers—a name often given to the fleet of a dozen or so—have become an institution. Although they're operated primarily to give pleasure to their paying passengers, the handsome vessels have enhanced the lives of their captains (who are generally owners as well), their crews, and those who watch from shore.

Schooner-watching is at its best during the two or three annual get-togethers when the vessels gather en masse in an anchorage. It's a sight to be remembered!

MERCANTILE
LOA: 78'0"   Beam: 21'5"
Modeled and built 1916 by Billings Bros., Little Deer Isle, Maine

LEWIS R. FRENCH
LOA: 64'6"   Beam: 18'6"
Modeled by A. & M. Gamage
Built 1871 by the French Bros., Christmas Cove, Maine

MARY DAY
LOA: 83'0"   Beam: 23'6"
Designed by Capt. Havilah Hawkins, Sr.
Built 1962 by Harvey F. Gamage, South Bristol, Maine

VICTORY CHIMES

A rare three-master

It'll be foggy tonight on Eggemoggin Reach on the Maine coast, where the cruise schooner *Victory Chimes* has chosen to anchor. A southeast wind blows the moist, tropical Gulf Stream air in over the chilly coastal waters. That damp air, now cooled, condenses to form fog, a frequent, sometimes dreaded, but eerily beautiful summer visitor. Bring in a west wind and the fog goes away. Heat up the damp air with midday sunshine and there's a scale-up—a temporary clearing—even without a change in the wind.

Although schooner passengers appreciate the awesome beauty of evenings such as this, they're not likely to enjoy a long spell of thick fog. They have only a week, after all, to see as much as possible of the coastline's beauty. The schooner will do her part by moving to a different anchorage every night, rigging awnings over the deck, turning out sumptuous meals, and providing a cheery cabin. Mother Nature, less predictable, bears watching—not a bad way to pass the time when she puts on a show like that in the left-hand photo. With a little luck, the wind will come west, the sky will clear, and an equally dramatic, different kind of coastal beauty can be enjoyed.

LOA: 132'0"   Beam: 24'0"
Modeled and built 1900 by J.M.C. Moore,
*   Bethel, Delaware*
Photographed off Brooklin and Owls Head, Maine

NATHANIEL BOWDITCH

A salty William Hand schooner

This vessel is once again schooner-rigged and used for the pleasure of her passengers. In the beginning of her life back in 1922, she was built as a schooner-yacht. Her name then was *Ladona*, and she was owned by Homer Loring of Boston. Hobart Ford bought her in 1935 and renamed her *Jane Dore*—a name that stuck with her through her years as a patrol boat during World War II and as a commercial fishing dragger in the years that followed. Stripped of her tall sailing rig, laid out with a fish hold amidships, and equipped with a pilothouse, diesel engine, double drum winch, and other gear for fishing, this vessel proved her versatility for more than 20 years. Then, about 25 years ago a group called The American Practical Navigators bought her, made some extensive repairs and rearrangements, fitted her once more with a sailing rig, got the vessel approved by the Coast Guard to carry passengers for hire, and entered her in the cruise business. Her name became *Nathaniel Bowditch*.

Designer William Hand always liked a rugged hull in terms of both shape and construction. In 1921 he and Hodgdon Bros. produced the Arctic-exploration schooner *Bowdoin* for Donald B. MacMillan, a vessel that proved indisputably rugged in all ways. *Ladona*, a year later, was similar, so it's little wonder that an astute fisherman got the idea of converting her into a fishing vessel. That both she and *Bowdoin*—now owned by the Maine Maritime Academy—have survived and remain in good condition today is testament to both designer and builder.

LOA: 81'0"   Beam: 20'5"
Designed by William H. Hand, Jr.
Built 1922 by Hodgdon Bros., East Boothbay, Maine
Photographed in Penobscot Bay, Maine

Two Schooners on Penobscot Bay

What becomes of a retired wooden-hulled schooner that was built for labor-intensive dory fishing? Once fishermen no longer needed them, some lucky schooners were saved and at least one was put to use in Maine's windjammer trade. Over the years, that passenger-carrying fleet has included both converted fishing vessels like the *Adventure* (opposite, foreground) and schooners built new for the trade, like the *Mary Day* (background).

The *Adventure* was once a familiar sight among the beautiful islands of the Maine coast, operated out of Camden by Capt. Jim Sharp. She has since returned to her onetime home port of Gloucester, Massachusetts, to serve as a living monument to the great days of sail. Repainted the original black as she was in her earliest days of commercial fishing, *Adventure* is a rare attraction. Penobscot Bay's loss has become Gloucester's distinct gain.

ADVENTURE
LOA: 121'6"   Beam: 24'6"
Built 1926 by John F. James & Son, Essex, Massachusetts

MARY DAY
LOA: 83'0"   Beam: 23'6"
Designed by Capt. Havilah Hawkins, Sr.
Built 1962 by Harvey F. Gamage, South Bristol, Maine

WANDER BIRD

An ex-pilot schooner in her second century

Boasting a lifetime of adventures under sail, this ex-pilot schooner has also been a home afloat for more than 100 years. *Wander Bird* was built to feed and sleep a crew of five, plus up to 16 pilots who awaited inbound ships approaching the River Elbe off Germany's North Sea coast. After 43 years in that trade and a few years laid up, Warwick Tompkins and his family called the vessel home as they sailed her all over the world with paying passengers as crew. World War II ended her odyssey, but even during her subsequent years of idleness and deterioration in California, people often lived aboard the Sausalito-based derelict. A new life began in 1969, when Harold and Annaliese Sommer purchased *Wander Bird* and moved aboard. Their dedication was infectious, and by offering the 'Bird as a temporary home for volunteers, the Sommers created a kind of community project; over the next dozen years, the vessel underwent one of the most magnificent amateur restorations ever carried out anywhere.

LOA: 85'0"   Beam: 18'6"
Designed and built 1883 by H.A. Stucklen,
     Hamburg, Germany
Photographed on San Francisco Bay, California

ALCYONE

Based on the Gloucester fishing schooners

Furling a headsail from the end of a bowsprit isn't always as calm and dry as indicated in this view (facing page) of the schooner *Alcyone*. Usually there's no lee, such as is provided here by the Marin County hills of California, and by the time the light-weather sails start to come down in a freshening breeze, there's also some rearing and plunging and flying spray. Both *Alcyone* (named for a mythical daughter of Atlas) and her owners are comfortable no matter what the weather—whether at sea or in harbor. The famed Grand Banks fishing schooners of Gloucester, Massachusetts, inspired *Alcyone*'s design, yet she's a Pacific Northwest boat, having been built by Seattle's legendary Frank Prothero for his own use. For more than two decades, she was sailed from nearby Port Townsend and kept bandbox-perfect by the Hanke family. Lately, *Alcyone* has been put to work chartering up and down the West Coast, allowing her present (and very competent) owners, "Sugar" Flanagan and Leslie McNish, to continue with the proper kind of care while providing their guests with schooner sailing at its best.

LOA: 65'0"   Beam: 15'2"
Designed and built 1956 by Frank Prothero, Lake Union, Seattle, Washington
Photographed on San Francisco Bay, California and Puget Sound, Washington

ACTIV

A converted Danish trader

When hauling goods over roads became more efficient than transporting them by water, hundreds of traditional oak-hulled Danish traders found themselves up for sale at bargain prices, and romantics from all over flocked to Baltic waters for their own tall ships. Conversions tended to be extensive, and much of this outfitting for sea took place in and around Svendborg, Denmark. *Activ's* transformation took place there in the late 1970s, at the Trøense yard of Michael Kiersgaard. She arrived as a diesel-powered freighter (one of her last regular runs was carrying barley from farmlands to the Tuborg brewery in Copenhagen) and left as a German-owned and London-registered topsail schooner laid out for chartering in the Eastern Mediterranean. Even in her original form, with graceful sheer and round stern, *Activ* (then *Mona*) was unusually handsome. Now, given a tall rig with more than a dozen sails, and still kept in tiptop shape, the sight of her is arresting.

LOA: 96'6"   Beam: 23'0"
Designed and built 1951 by the Ring-Andersen Shipyard,
*   Svendborg, Denmark*
Photographed at Douarnenez, France

PRIDE OF BALTIMORE II

The latest Baltimore Clipper

At a working shipyard set up on the edge of Baltimore's revitalized Inner Harbor, 15 people in 15 months built this vessel to the point of launching in the spring of 1988. Seven months later, she was ready for sea. Her mission is to travel the world as an ambassador representing the state of Maryland, and thousands of visitors have already been aboard. The *Pride*'s first 8,000-mile passage was south into the Caribbean and the Gulf of Mexico, and her second one, of the same length, took her north through the Great Lakes. In the fall of 1991, she returned from a year and a half in Europe.

The building and sailing of traditional wooden vessels is fascinating work, with a new challenge at every turn. Over the past couple of decades the resurgence of interest in this kind of craft has allowed many young people to become proficient shipwrights, riggers, and deepwater seamen. These important skills, once on the brink of extinction, now survive and even flourish. *Pride of Baltimore II* embodies all this. Not only is she exceptionally well-built and impeccably maintained, but she is sailed and managed with competence and flair.

LOA: 96'10"   Beam: 26'0"
Designed by Thomas C. Gillmer
Built 1988 by Capt. Peter Boudreau, Baltimore, Maryland
Photographed off Brooklin, Maine

CHAPTER IV

OPEN BOATS

Daysailers, rowboats, and canoes make up the bulk of this chapter. They are the affordable craft that can be stored at home, trailered at least for short distances over the road, and can provide more hours of use for less cost than any other watercraft. Because they will fit inside garages and other available storage areas, small open boats often escape the long exposure to harmful weathering that tends to shorten the lives of larger craft. And, simply because of their size, the painting, cleaning, and repairing is less of a chore.

Coastal cruising is a real possibility in boats that are no larger than this. A deck, if there is one, or an awning of some kind if there isn't, keeps off the dew and rain while you use the floorboards for sleeping. Even the smallest can take you on an adventure during the day, and be light enough to haul up on the shore beside your sleeping bag at night.

But if there's only an hour or two to satisfy those spur-of-the-moment callings during perfect wind and weather, you have a fine chance with these little boats, since with any of them you're underway in a jiffy. I suppose, on second thought, the sandbagger *Puffin*, the felucca *Nuovo Mondo*, and the French-built *Narvik* may be exceptions because of the size and complexity of the rigs they carry. *Pixie*, shown here, carries a good-sized spread of sail; nevertheless, she is still a practical boat for short bursts of single-handed sailing.

Designed before the turn of the century for use on the notoriously choppy waters of Buzzards Bay, the Herreshoff 15 (named, in the understated custom of the times, for its waterline length) provides a sporty ride even today. A lightweight hull with outside ballast and plenty of sail area gives the boat its lively performance. The centerboard allows sailing in shallow waters, and, even with an outside ballast keel of cast lead, *Pixie*'s watertight compartment (formed in the bow by a bulkhead) keeps her safely afloat if capsized. The Herreshoff Mfg. Co. used a building method that was particularly efficient when applied to several boats of a single design, and, next to the 12½-footer shown on the following page, this was the yard's most popular model. Some 100 were built between 1898 and 1927. Minor differences between boats from one racing fleet to another resulted in a variety of class names: Buzzards Bay 15, Newport 15, and Watch Hill 15. The name "Herreshoff 15" covers all.

PIXIE, a lively Watch Hill 15 class sloop   *LOA: 24'6"*   *Beam: 6'8"*   *Designed by N.G. Herreshoff*
Built 1922 by the Herreshoff Mfg. Co., Bristol, Rhode Island   *Photographed off Noank, Connecticut*

TWO 12½S: A HAVEN AND A HERRESHOFF

The Herreshoff Buzzards Bay 12½ (so designated because of its waterline length) has been in production in various forms for more than 75 years—a record that may be unequaled. The first batch of twenty boats came out in the winter of 1914–15, and the Herreshoff Mfg. Co. continued turning out these lovely little daysailers for three decades—until the count reached 360 boats in 1943. Through a subsequent licensing agreement, and the ultimate sale of the building rights when the Herreshoff yard closed after World War II, construction continued—in wood until the 1950s, and then in fiberglass. Today, the same basic boat is still manufactured in three fiberglass versions—the Bullseye, the Doughdish, and the H-12.

Also being built in wood on a more limited basis are Haven 12½s, a recent design based on the Herreshoff boats, but made shallower—and thus beachable and trailerable—through the use of a centerboard. *Petrel*, shown here in the shop nearing completion, is the first of these boats. Three inches more beam compensates for 12″ less draft and with these changes *Petrel* has proven equal to the original Herreshoff boats in speed, stability, and handling. In her design and construction, looking "right" was as important a goal as sailing well. This was achieved by diligently adhering to Herreshoff's proportions and shapes for each piece of wood that went into her.

BLUE BELL, *a Buzzards Bay 12 ½ class sloop*
LOA: 15′10″   Beam: 5′10″
Designed by N.G. Herreshoff
Built 1928 by Herreshoff Mfg. Co., Bristol, Rhode Island
Photographed in Eggemoggin Reach near Brooklin, Maine

PETREL, *a Haven 12 ½ class sloop (lower right)*
LOA: 16′0″   Beam: 6′1″
Designed by Joel White
Built 1986 by Maynard Bray, Doug Hylan, and
   Joel White
Photographed at Brooklin, Maine

THE BEETLE CAT

A little gaff-rigger with lots of friends

For a glimpse at small boatbuilding carried out as it should be, you shouldn't miss a visit to the Beetle Cat shop of Concordia Boat Yard in South Dartmouth, Massachusetts. It's a production shop where a crew of three or four turn out about 30 of these 12' gaff-rigged catboats each winter. The work is fast and efficient, yet of the highest quality. There's a well-worn template for nearly every piece, and the whole operation takes place without a wasted movement. It's an inspiring sight. To lie where they're supposed to on a Beetle Cat's ever-changing shape, some of the planks have to be sawn out with very distinct and deliberate curves along their edges. All the planks have to be tapered in width. They are made of white cedar, a tree which has a tapering and sometimes curved trunk; the natural shapes of its live-edge boards can be used to advantage in the planking of a small boat. Cedar has other advantages as well: it's long-lived, it's light in weight, it's easy to work, and it will stay put after it's fastened. And, as you'd notice upon entering this shop, it smells simply wonderful.

Besides being fun to own and sail (especially for children), Beetle Cats have always been reasonably priced. They're a bargain, really, and that's why the demand for them held up during the 1960s and early '70s when fiberglass was the rage. In fact, Beetle Cat production has been going on pretty steadily since the first one rolled out of John Beetle's shop in 1921. Several thousand have been built, mostly for the New England racing fleets.

LOA: 12'4"   *Beam: 6'0"*
Designed by John Beetle
Built by the Concordia Co., South Dartmouth,
    Massachusetts
Photographed at South Dartmouth, Massachusetts, and
    Brooklin, Maine

PUFFIN

A new sandbagger designed in Civil War days

As is evident, *Puffin*'s sailspread would do for a boat twice as long, and keeping this low, shallow craft from capsizing sometimes requires knee-jerk sailing skill. With wind, each of the five crew members has a task. Besides steering, there's jibsheet-trimming (to ease the helm and to ease the whole boat, in fact, during a big puff), a long mainsheet to tend, and more than two dozen 35-pound sandbags to be carried across the cockpit and piled on the windward deck at each tack. Until about 1880, yachting was relatively unsophisticated, with New York Bay as its epicenter and sandbaggers like *Puffin* as the accepted type of small racing craft. *Puffin* herself was launched in Maine from The Rockport Apprenticeshop 110 years later, but to a Civil War-era design. She has already proven great fun to sail, and, as was advertised for the sandbaggers of old, offers "to breed a host of bold, hardy, and skilled sailors." Now if only more sandbaggers could be built so they could be raced together....

LOA: 18′0″   Beam: 8′0″
Designed by A. Cary Smith
Built 1990 by The Rockport Apprenticeshop,
    Rockport, Maine
Photographed at Rockport

NUOVO MONDO

A San Francisco felucca replica

Once turned out by the hundreds for immigrant Italian fishermen, boats like this San Francisco felucca were based on the native craft of their Mediterranean homeland. Unfortunately, the details of how feluccas were built and used were never documented. Scholars tended to shun both the boats and their owners as unworthy subjects, and the fishermen themselves were far too busy eking out a living to have left much behind in the way of records. With that way of life now vanished, we wish someone had paid more attention.

Some photographs do survive, however, from the late 19th century, when feluccas lined the San Francisco waterfront. And a single derelict was rescued by the Maritime Museum there. Using such evidence, and a few other scanty sources, the museum had *Nuovo Mondo* built as a way of relearning, firsthand, some of what has been lost. The Bay's brisk winds and notoriously turbulent waters prove ideal in pushing both hull and lateen rig to their limits.

LOA: 18'6"   Beam: 7'0"
Built 1987 by Larry Hitchcock, San Francisco, California
Photographed on San Francisco Bay

ROBERT H. BAKER

A clipper-bowed gaff-rigged dayboat

This little packet with her clipper bow and trailboards, simple gaff rig, sweet sheerline, and low bulwarks embodies, in miniature, the character of coastal New England working watercraft before the days of engines, synthetic materials, and high-tech equipment. The *Robert H. Baker* is a craft steeped in tradition, yet one not easily categorized. She came from the drawing board of her namesake, the late Bob Baker, who claimed he was "just having fun" when he designed her. Bob's knowledge of traditional design elements was so keen, however, and his sense of proportion so finely tuned, that some outstanding work emerged even when he was only playing around with a pencil. Baker's designs look "right" even to the most discriminating eye. Here's one of them: a sloop built by The Rockport (Maine) Apprenticeshop as a tribute to her designer—a man who devoted his life to the study, design, and restoration of traditional small craft.

LOA: 20'2"   Beam: 7'6"
Designed by Robert H. Baker
Built 1985 by The Rockport Apprenticeshop,
*   Rockport, Maine*
Photographed at Rockport

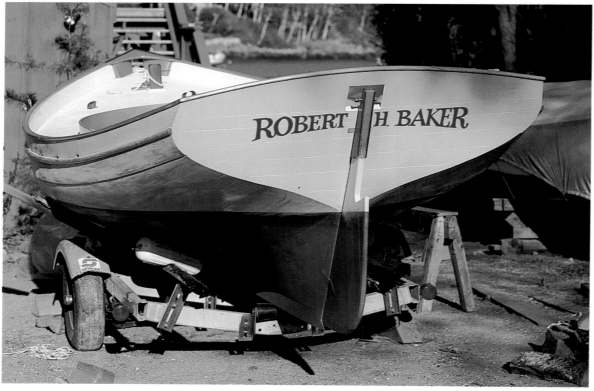

NARVIK

A vaquelotte from the Normandy coast of France

Although she's only 16' long, *Narvik* is quite a ship—with full keel, inside ballast, and a two-masted lug rig. She can be sculled or rowed, of course, but she carries a small Lister diesel in her present role as a representative of the Association of Maritime Heritage of Normandy. With no boom and no deck (except way forward), and the masts stepped near the bow and the stern, there's ample space for the fishing that once was her trade.

Narvik is native to the Normandy region of France, but these photographs were taken farther south in the Bay of Douarnenez during the area's wonderful quadrennial festival that celebrates traditional boats from all over Europe. In 1988, when these pictures were taken, some 750 of them sailed and raced by day, then gathered in harbor at night. The pastoral farmland in the background here could convince almost anyone that time had truly been turned back.

LOA: 16'9"   Beam: 6'11"
Built 1953 in St. Vaast, La Hague, France
Photographed at Douarnenez, France

BAHAMA DINGHIES OF THE ANDROS ISLANDS

When you set out to build a boat and your choice of materials and tools is limited, you make the design a simple one. Look at these Bahama dinghies. Their sails are laced to the mast instead of attached with hoops or metal slides, the masts have no standing rigging, and there's enough of an external keel so no centerboard is needed. Their big rigs demand stability, which they get from a few beach stones in the bilge or the weight of the crew hiking out on a short plank jammed under the lee seat riser and resting on the windward rail.

The fishermen near Lisbon Creek on the island of Andros have always had simple boats, built locally—boats that are roughly finished but functionally beautiful. Their loose-footed, secondhand sails are inefficient, but because they have so much area, there's plenty of chance for speed and excitement.

For most people a dinghy is a pleasure craft; but these are used primarily for commercial fishing. The weight and stability of the dinghy allows the fisherman to lean over the side with a glass-bottomed bucket and hook up conch with a long-handled "grabber." Crawfish, sponges, turtles, and other bottom-dwellers are harvested by dinghy as well.

Throughout the Bahamas are dinghies like these that have been rigged for sailing—fitted with a mast, boom, sail, and rudder to reach fishing grounds farther from home. A fisherman is quite apt to build his own boat, modeling her by eye as he goes along, so no two are exactly alike, and there is sometimes considerable difference in speed. Regattas—there are several each year—test which dinghy is fastest and also give owners an occasional break from the workaday routine.

LOA: 12'-13'   Beam: about 5'
Modeled and built by Bernard Longley (boat under sail)
*   and other Andros Island builders, Bahamas*
Photographed at Lisbon Creek and South Andros Island

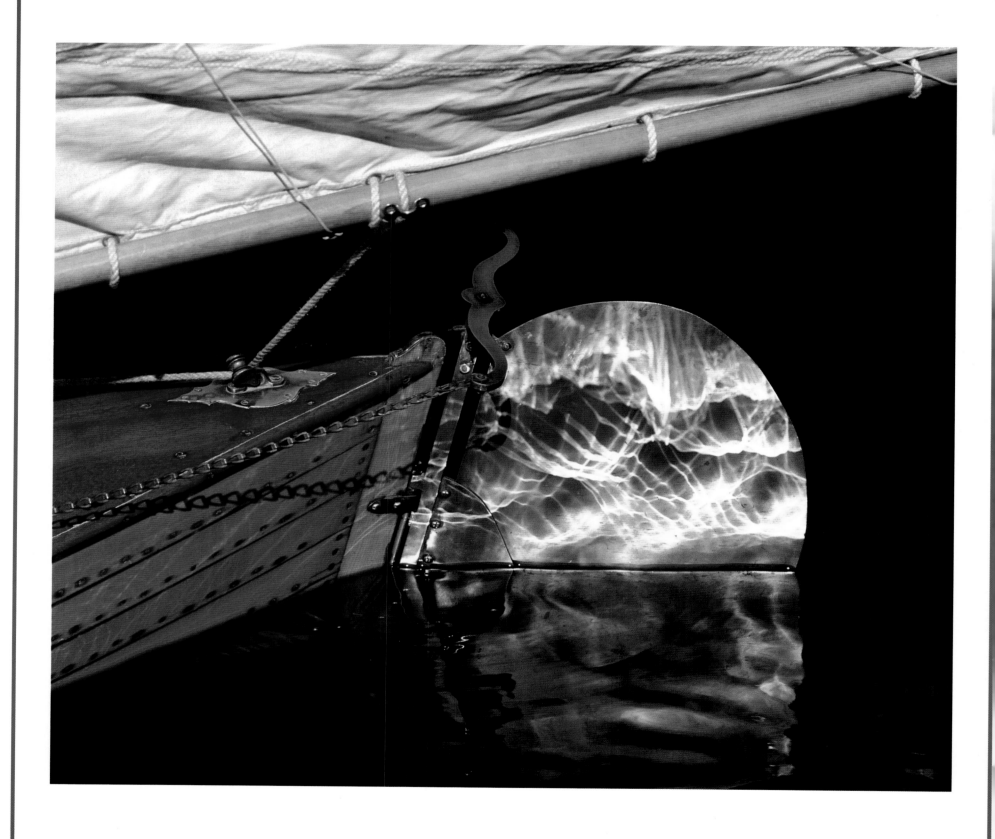

TWILITE

A decked sailing canoe of lapstrake cedar

*T*wilite is a recently built version of a Vesper-model sailing canoe. For shallow water, her bronze rudder can be raised as it is here, and her fan-type metal centerboard can be pulled up as well. Either under sail or paddle, steering is by foot pedal.

A hundred years ago, such decked canoes of lapstrake cedar construction were turned out assembly-line fashion at surprisingly affordable prices. Many of these charming, exquisitely built one-person boats were bought by adventurers for use in exploring the wilderness by river, lake, or stream. They were paddled kayak-style, and some, like *Twilite*, were fitted out for sailing, usually as lug-rigged ketches. You and the boat might go by railroad from the city to a good starting place. Then, if you planned it right, you could pick up the train again near the end of your cruise to make the trip home. For anyone who enjoyed his own company, it was an ideal way to spend leisure time.

LOA: 15′0″   Beam: 2′6″
Designed by Gibson and Rushton
Built 1974 by Everett Smith, Canton, New York
Photographed in Western Massachusetts

OPEN BOATS

ADIRONDACK GUIDEBOAT

Built light for easy carrying

Summer recreation a century or so ago for a New York sportsman who could afford it was often a trip to the cool Adirondack region of his home state. Once there, he would hire a local guide to take him fishing. With few exceptions, his boat was the exquisite Adirondack guideboat, a modern reproduction of which is shown here. There could be as many as three heavy people and considerable gear in one of these 14' boats, so their hulls had to be buoyant and easily rowed. Also, the frequent portages between the many lakes made it necessary for the boats to be light and portable. Their planking, although only about ¼" thick, provides much of the strength because the individual strakes are beveled, lapped, and fastened together to form the perfectly smooth skin. As often happens when people with good taste and money mingle with those who are unusually skilled at building fine things, objects are created that not only are perfect in their function but also are works of art. The Adirondack guideboat was such a creation.

LOA: 14'6"   Beam: 3'0"
Modeled by William Vassar
Built 1983 by John Breitenbach, Jr., Silver Bay,
 New York
Photographed on Lake George, New York

EIDER

A tiny ultralight canoe by Tom Hill

A truly lightweight canoe is a wonderful thing: it can be stored at home, thrown onto or into the car (this one fits entirely inside a station wagon), and carried to the water. You can, all by yourself with little effort, lug it across a stretch of land between one body of water and the next. If the canoe is elegant inside and out, which *Eider* is, you can enjoy what it is as well as what it does. High-grade mahogany plywood forms this canoe's hull, being cut into overlapped, glued planks. So built, there is no need for internal framing, and the resulting round-bottomed boat is unusually easy to maintain. Another advantage is plywood's dimensional stability—when the canoe is stored outside, the planks won't shrink in the sun, so everything stays watertight. Altogether, the material, construction, and design are in complete harmony, just as in these pictures the young paddler, the canoe, and the sheltered water all combine to make a perfect match.

LOA: 9'8"   Beam: 2'2"
Designed by Carl Bauch
Built 1983 by Thomas J. Hill, Charlotte, Vermont
Photographed in Brooklin, Maine

RAIL BIRD SKIFF

For gunning in the Delaware Bay marshes

Although shown here on a pond during a recent duck hunters' meet, rail bird skiffs like this, a century ago, would have been found throughout the backwaters of Delaware Bay, south of Philadelphia, where the shooting of rail birds was once a brisk endeavor. (Now, rail hunting centers only around the Maurice River.) Twice in the course of each day, high tide submerged the dense wild rice that the birds fed on before the area succumbed to industrialization. The birds would lose their cover, and their habitat would become accessible to boats. For a couple of hours during the daytime highs, hunters navigated the marshes in narrow, easily poled, double-ended skiffs and duckers. The gunner (often a city "sport" who paid for the privilege) crouched in the bow, ready to shoot at the first sign of a fluttering bird. The boat's owner, known as the pusher, stood high on the after deck and propelled the boat with a long boat-length pole, hoping to sneak up on some of the robin-sized rail birds and drive them into flight.

LOA: 15'4"   Beam: 3'4"
Designed by Vannaman & Blew
Built 1981 by Philadelphia Maritime Museum
Photographed in Southern New Jersey

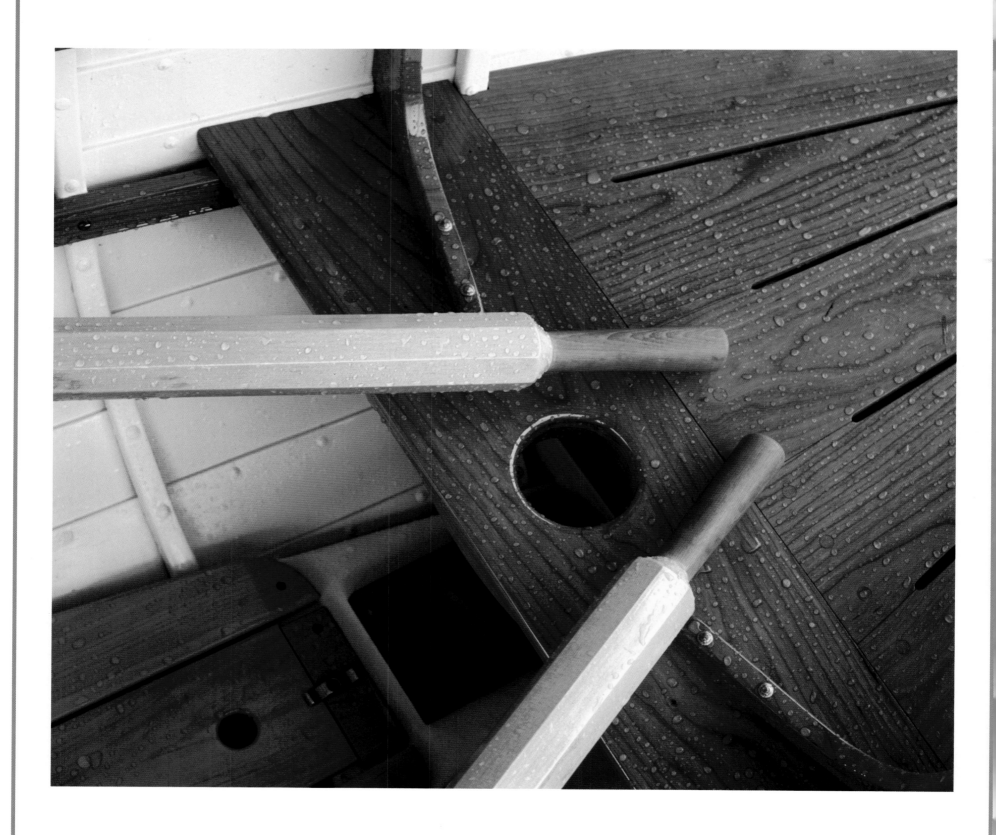

ZEPHYR

An elegant Whitehall pulling boat

Whitehall pulling boats are among the most beautiful of all small craft. But, as with any small open boat, the structural detailing often makes the difference between what looks "right" and what looks "wrong" (or perhaps "clumsy"). Each element has to be pared down proportionately to the point where it has sufficient, but not excessive, strength. If you appreciate structural design as art as well as function, you'll have difficulty finding a better example than the 16'9" *Zephyr* shown here. Look at the graceful shape of the seat knees and backrest, the beaded corners of the seat riser, and the star carved into the mast step under the seat. Yet she's not overdone—a common mistake of some craftsmen who get carried away emphasizing their use of wood. The wood accented by varnish in *Zephyr* is beautiful cherry, the rest of her is lightweight cedar and strong oak, painted. Like the century-old boat at Mystic Seaport on which she was based, *Zephyr* has oarlocks on folding outriggers and a sliding seat—altogether, a very special boat.

LOA: 16'9"   Beam: 3'9'
Built 1982 by Ken's Boatshop, Seaford, New York
Photographed at Mystic Seaport Museum,
*   Mystic, Connecticut*

NEW MEADOWS ROWBOAT

From the schooner Isaac H. Evans

Rowing is fun—especially in the morning calm before the rest of the world awakens, and especially if you have a good wooden boat under you. There is a sense of quiet and a sense of beauty. And the beauty comes not only from surroundings like pastoral Pulpit Harbor on North Haven Island in Maine, but from the form and structure of the boat that is taking you on this wonderful row. No small boat of synthetic materials could possibly awaken one to such an appreciation of his environment; fiberglass or aluminum would simply be out of place in this natural setting.

Early-morning rows are not uncommon for this boat because she comes from the cruise schooner *Isaac H. Evans*, whose passengers, aboard for a week's sail on the Maine coast, can make use of her if they're so inclined and if they've learned the rudiments of rowing.

Like all good rowing craft of her size, this New Meadows pulling boat (named for the river from which she originated) has two rowing stations. Both can be used at the same time, with another person and another pair of oars, or either station may be used individually, allowing a single oarsman a chance to sit where his weight will best trim the boat. Here, she's riding just about perfectly with the rower using the aft station.

LOA: 14'0"   Beam: 4'3"
Rebuilt 1975 by Capt. Douglas K. Lee (original builder unknown)
Photographed at Pulpit Harbor, North Haven, Maine

THE DOWNEAST PEAPODS OF JIM STEELE

Peapods were developed for lobstering close to shore in the days when inshore catches were abundant; the early working pods were wider on the waterline than those shown here. These peapods, of which well over 100 have been built by Jim Steele, are finely shaped for easy recreational rowing, and at that they are an unqualified success. Being symmetrical, they work well in either direction, the end that is loaded heaviest can be considered the stern; so rowed, the boat has sufficient drag to her keel to track well. Despite being undecked, the peapod is noted for its seaworthiness. Riding like a seabird on the water, it will rise to surprisingly big oncoming seas without taking water, or even spray, over the rails. As other small boats and even other peapods go, this model is hard to beat for good looks. From any angle, including the two we're able to enjoy in the single view at the bottom right, it's strikingly handsome.

Hauled on the beach along with a Jim Steele peapod under a rising moon is a Nutshell pram, her lugsail still set in a gentle headwind. Long into the night, when this spur-of-the-moment supper on the shore comes to a close, the two boats will be ready to carry their passengers noiselessly home—the pram under sail, the peapod under oars. It's times like this that small boats demonstrate their worth!

LOA: 13′6″   Beam: 4′6″
Designed by Capt. Havilah H. Hawkins, Sr.
Built from 1962 to present by James F. Steele,
    Brooklin, Maine
Photographed in Brooklin

CHAPTER V

SAILING YACHTS

In days gone by, yachts of this size had a paid crew to help sail them; now, the assistance is more apt to come from friends or even from passengers who pay for the privilege of experiencing life aboard one of these so-called "gold-platers."

Private ownership of a large and finely-finished wooden yacht, with its varnish, gloss paint, teak decks, and sophisticated rigging, is a monumental obligation requiring time, talent, and money in seemingly endless amounts. Covered storage is the only reliable method of maintenance-free preservation, but because of their size, that kind of treatment is out of the question for most of these boats. Thus, it comes down to an organized program of routine maintenance, carried on daily. My hat is off to the owners and crews who do this, for their task is unending, even though there's great satisfaction in that kind of stewardship.

Yachts like those shown here are really national treasures. As such, they are every bit as worthy for their design, finely crafted construction and finish, and often for their history, as are the privately-owned, land-based structures which we readily designate as historic and provide public support for. Why, at the very least, there aren't similar incentives and advantages available to the owners of large classic yachts is hard to figure. Although the yachts shown here are now in good hands, they tend to be the exception rather than the norm—and very few of these graceful beauties are being built now, or will ever be again. As a society, we need to do more to help boats like *Stormy Weather* survive.

In 1934, when *Stormy Weather* was launched, the style of ocean racers was changing rapidly from fisherman-type schooners to narrower, more sophisticated yawls carrying all of their ballast outside as a cast-lead keel. The transition had received a big boost from *Stormy Weather*'s prototype *Dorade*, in 1931, when, as the smallest and seemingly most fragile contestant in the transatlantic race from Newport, Rhode Island, to Plymouth, England, she trounced the entire fleet and went on to win the 1931 and 1933 Fastnet Races. Then it was *Stormy Weather*'s turn. With Rod Stephens as skipper, *Stormy Weather* enjoyed equal success in a 3,100-mile race from Newport, Rhode Island, to Bergen, Norway, in 1935 and in the subsequent Fastnet. In 1936, she won her class in the Bermuda Race, and the next year she cleaned up in the Miami-Nassau Race. *Stormy Weather* and *Dorade* established the yawl as the standard rig for ocean racers for the next two decades.

How fine it is that, at least for now, this swift pair is still well kept and sailing! The Pacific Northwest is now *Dorade*'s home, while *Stormy Weather*, shown here in the Antigua-to-Guadeloupe Race, carries on the legend in Caribbean waters.

STORMY WEATHER, an ocean-racing yawl   *LOA: 53'11"   Beam: 12'6"   Designed by Sparkman & Stephens, Inc. Built 1934 by Henry B. Nevins, Inc., City Island, New York   Photographed in the Leeward Islands of the Caribbean*

MALABAR II

An early Alden schooner

Everyone loves a schooner, it seems, especially one as handsome in hull and rig as *Malabar II*. Basic qualities, such as grace, proportion, strength, simplicity, economy, and practicality, are so evident that second looks and complimentary remarks come even from nonsailors. And if *Malabar II* looks natural in her element, it's because John G. Alden, her designer, was a natural himself. With little technical education, he grew in stature to lead the field when it came to designing fast ocean-racing schooners. A natural sailor as well, Alden campaigned, with almost predictable success, a new Malabar schooner each year (there were 10 in all) from 1921 until the rig went out of style near the end of the decade. Although *Malabar II*, shown here, dates back to 1922, she was given a second lease on life in 1954 with a brand-new hull carefully built by Elmer Collemer, whose Camden, Maine, shop was only minutes from this schooner's original Thomaston building site. Now home-ported at Martha's Vineyard and cared for by her owners, Jim and Ginny Lobdell, *Malabar II* enjoys a seasonal romp Down East and has been captured on film as she reaches down Eggemoggin Reach—naturally.

LOA: 41'6"   Beam: 11'3"
Designed by John G. Alden
Built 1922 by Charles A. Morse, Thomaston, Maine
Photographed on Eggemoggin Reach, Maine

WHEN AND IF

General Patton's Alden schooner

When "the boys" returned to the U.S. at the close of World War I and took up ocean racing as a peacetime adventure, the wholesome schooner-yacht developed out of the then-common Gloucester-type fishing schooner and became immensely popular. Designers such as William Hand and John Alden led the way with their salty new creations, and names like "Malabar schooner" and "Alden schooner" came into being and would never be forgotten. As the 1920s turned into the 1930s, however, the schooner-yacht was joined in offshore racing by more and more sloops, cutters, and yawls and gradually lost favor to these more aerodynamically efficient rigs.

When and If dates from 1939 and is one of the last of the Alden schooners to be built. General George S. Patton, then a colonel in the Army, ordered her with the same prospect of adventure that had fired the imaginations of the returning soldiers 20 years earlier. This time, however, the idea was a round-the-world trip—"when and if" his military career allowed it. But the trip never materialized—Patton's death at the close of World War II ended his dream.

This beautiful schooner was considered a total loss, at least by the insurer, after breaking loose and smashing upon the Manchester, Massachusetts, ledges in the fall of 1990. She'll survive and sail again, however, thanks to the energy, dedication, and dreams of her new owners.

LOA: 63'5"   Beam: 15'0"
Designed by John G. Alden
Built 1939 by F.F. Pendleton, Wiscasset, Maine
Photographed on Penobscot Bay, Maine

VOYAGER

A knuckle-bowed Alden schooner

What should you do when your wooden boat gets old, tired, and worn-out? Building a new hull for her is one answer, and that is precisely what the owner of *Voyager* set about to do. He found that her rig was still good, and so were her engine, her fittings, her interior, and her ballast keel. Her problems, underscored by rather extreme leakage when under sail, were almost wholly with her hull. Of course the hull could have been repaired—nearly anything can, given the money and time—but because it had been fastened together for the most part with iron, which in 45 years had rusted badly, even a major repair didn't seem practical. Thus, *Voyager* was taken to a good boatyard, her original drawings dusted off, and work was commenced on a brand-new hull. One just like what she had, so that a transfer could be made of all the salvageable hardware, gear, etc.

When finished, *Voyager* was as strong and good as she had been back in 1930 when first built. She no longer leaked, she had the market value of a newly-built craft as well as the nostalgic appeal of an old one, and the cost of doing the job was within reasonable limits.

The picture on the facing page was taken during the Opera House Cup race in Nantucket a few years ago when there was a good breeze blowing and a good sea running—just the kind of weather these husky Alden schooners were designed for.

LOA: 50'6"   Beam: 14'3"
Designed by John G. Alden
Built 1929 by Charles A. Morse & Son,
    Thomaston, Maine
Photographed off Nantucket, Massachusetts, and on
    Eggemoggin Reach, Maine

SPARTAN

A New York 50

Behind these waves is a truly great boat. She's *Spartan*, one of maybe two surviving 72-foot racing sloops built in 1913 for New York Yacht Club members and known as the New York 50' class after their waterline length. Nine were built to a design of Nathanael G. Herreshoff by the Herreshoff Manufacturing Co., in Bristol, Rhode Island. *Spartan* is a marconi yawl now, but all the New York 50s originally carried a big gaff-headed mainsail of about 2,000 square feet, a club topsail, and three headsails. The New York 50s are stunningly beautiful craft and, in my opinion, were one of the best creations of their great designer. *Spartan* broke her mast a few minutes after these sailing pictures were taken, and was hauled out for a complete restoration at the end of that 1980 season. Sixty-seven years is a long time for any boat to be around, and she's not always had an easy time of it, having spent several years in a marginal charter operation with not enough revenue to keep her up properly. But if the work on her resumes after the recent hiatus and continues with the same high standards with which it was started, *Spartan* will come out of it as good as new.

LOA: 72'0"   Beam: 14'6"
Designed by N.G. Herreshoff
Built 1913 by Herreshoff Mfg. Co., Bristol, Rhode Island
Photographed off Nantucket, Massachusetts and in
    Clinton, Connecticut

MERRY DANCER

A sloop by Fife

Merry Dancer—a boat most appropriately named—heads toward the rough English Channel at sundown. At her helm is a new owner, sailing her for the first time. There's a good breeze blowing, so he has wisely rolled a deep reef into the mainsail to keep things under control in the dark of night. Although she's more than 50 years old, Merry Dancer should be able to take almost any weather and not come to harm because she was designed and built by William Fife of Fairlie, Scotland, one of the best builders ever.

Merry Dancer is framed with good oak, planked with the best mahogany available, and fastened with long-lasting copper rivets. Her decks are of laid teak and her cabin and trim are also teak. In spite of her age, her topside seams don't show because planks have been joined together with wedges, fitted and glued into the seams, as well as fastened to the frames in the usual manner. Fife-designed boats are all beautiful, and they're prized by their owners as being top-of-the-line in the world of wooden boats.

LOA: 51'8"   Beam: 11'0"
Designed by W. & R.B. Fife
Built 1938 by Wm. Fife & Son, Fairlie, Scotland
Photographed in the Solent off Southampton, England

INISMARA

A Scottish sloop

Before rating rules changed the prevailing style to light-displacement, high-sided, shallow-bodied, and wedge-shaped "machines," and before the high tooling costs of synthetic materials gave us hundreds of look-alike "product" boats, many wooden state-of-the-art racer/cruisers of the 1960s looked much like *Inismara*. They were relatively narrow and deep—which, along with outside ballast, made them self-righting, even in a storm sea; they were steady on the helm but still could maneuver in tight situations; and they had balanced ends and were heavy enough to give a predictable ride whatever the weather. Low cabins and high-cut sails allowed 360-degree visibility. I like to think such boats will always be considered good boats, no matter what the prevailing style or racing measurement rule. Certainly I know that the folks aboard *Inismara* feel they're on the perfect craft for enjoying the lovely Scottish landscape as it flashes by.

LOA: 41'6"   Beam: 9'9"
Designed by James McGruer
Built 1963 by McGruer & Co., Ltd., Clynder,
*   Dunbarton, Scotland*
Photographed on Gareloch, Scotland

SERENITY AND DEFIANCE

A pair of Peterson schooners

The graceful proportions of a coasting schooner have always appealed to romantics, and there have been many dreamers who imagined themselves with a smaller version of one of these old-time vessels outfitted as a yacht—a craft that would be practical in everyday use. Murray Peterson had this dream and was able to do something about it. His first personal schooner-yacht, called *Coaster*, came out in 1931 to a design worked out by him that was complete to the last detail. She was indeed a beauty and always a welcome sight in any company. He designed two more, *Coaster II* and *Coaster III*, for himself and when the war was over he drew up others, all of which had a charm of their own that sailors and nonsailors alike find irresistible.

In spite of their small size, Peterson schooners are real little ships. They are fitted out just like old-time coasting schooners, with catheads, trailboards, anchor windlasses, fidded topmasts and all. This could be said of many "character boats," but the thing that makes *Serenity*, *Defiance*, and the other Peterson schooners so appealing is the exquisite proportioning of all the pieces that make them up.

SERENITY
LOA: 36'8"   Beam: 11'2"
Designed by Murray G. Peterson
Built 1964 by Malcolm H. Brewer, Camden, Maine
Photographed at Camden, Maine

DEFIANCE
LOA: 45'0"   Beam: 13'10"
Designed by Murray G. Peterson
Built 1960 by Paul E. Luke, East Boothbay, Maine
Photographed in Fishers Island Sound

NEITH

A flush-deck sloop by Herreshoff

Little matter that you can't see outside when you're inside this flush-decked sloop. You can keep your eyes occupied for hours examining *Neith*'s exquisitely proportioned deck framing with its narrow swept decking and diagonal strapping, the cast-iron hanging knees that connect deckbeams to hull frames, the raised-panel bulkheads and partitions, doors, and drawers, the stanchion-supported shelf rails, the overhead skylight, and even the tufted velour cushions. If your eyes tell you, however, that what they see doesn't look the same age as the 86-year-old *Neith*, they're quite correct. When restoration began several years ago, *Neith* was in tough shape—requiring, among other things, all-new hull planking and decking. The joinerwork shown here had to be constructed anew as well, each piece carefully made to duplicate its original counterpart. The resulting ambience, as well as the finely crafted detail, makes being aboard *Neith* an unforgettable privilege.

LOA: 52'10"   Beam: 10'6"
Designed by N.G. Herreshoff
Built 1907 by Herreshoff Mfg. Co., Bristol, Rhode Island
Photographed at Noank, Connecticut, and Long Island
  Sound

ASTRA

A J-class sloop

There aren't many 115-foot sloops in the world, and few sailing yachts of any size handsomer than Astra. In 1937, the highly esteemed sailor and author Uffa Fox wrote that *Astra*'s designer, Charles Nicholson, had created in her a masterpiece whose lines would serve as an inspiration for all time. That accolade is as true today as it was then, and the sweet sheer, delicately curving bow, and subtly rounded forward sections that show here underscore Nicholson's skill.

Although planked and decked with wood, *Astra*'s hull is too big and too highly stressed to have a traditional wooden skeleton, so her keel, frames, deckbeams, and other key members are made of steel—what is known as composite construction. Before World War II, this was a standard building method for large yachts like *Astra*, the steel providing the necessary strength and the wooden skin producing the smooth topsides and nonskid deck.

LOA: 115'0"   Beam: 20'2"
Designed by Charles E. Nicholson
Built 1928 by Camper & Nicholson, Gosport,
*   Hampshire, England*
Photographed off Newport, Rhode Island

ATHENE

A yawl-rigged ocean racer

By 1937, when *Athene* was launched as *Elizabeth McCaw* for tobacco magnate R.J. Reynolds, both her designer, Olin Stephens, and her builder, the Nevins yard, had established reputations as the best in their fields. Wisely recognizing the superior skill and craftsmanship that created this classic ocean-racing yawl, all her subsequent owners have avoided major alterations. Thus *Athene* is an unusually fortunate yacht: fully appreciated, properly maintained, and still nearly 100-percent original. For three decades, *Athene*'s home has been San Francisco. There, where change occurs all around her in the blink of an eye, this yawl symbolizes the basic virtues of hand-wrought substance, timeless beauty, and thoughtful, steady care. May *Athene* thrive as well during her second half-century as she did during her first!

LOA: 63'4"   Beam: 13'10"
Designed by Sparkman & Stephens, Inc.
Built 1937 by Henry B. Nevins, Inc., City Island,
  New York
Photographed on San Francisco Bay

MYA AND NIPANTUCK

A schooner and a yawl off Newport, Rhode Island

The sky was mostly overcast when the sun briefly burst through to produce this dramatic lighting at the "right" time—when the schooner *Mya* and the yawl *Nipantuck* were looking their very best. Competing in the first annual Classic Yacht Regatta in 1980, sponsored by Newport's Museum of Yachting, they were racing in a fleet of nearly 100 other wooden beauties. The windward turning mark had been rounded and both boats had just gotten their off-the-wind staysails up and drawing. (Spinnakers weren't allowed in this race to be fair to the boats that didn't have them.) The Regatta's organizers continue to stress that a challenging all-out competition is secondary to the idea of bringing together as many classics as possible and getting them out sailing. Interest and appreciation are stimulated among owners and spectators alike, and each September the boats put on an elegant display in Newport Harbor.

MYA
LOA: 49'10"   Beam: 12'1"
Designed by the Concordia Co.
Built 1940 by Duxbury Boat Yard, Inc., Duxbury,
    Massachusetts

NIPANTUCK
LOA: 45'0"   Beam: 12'1"
Designed by Sparkman & Stephens, Inc.
Built 1946 by Henry B. Nevins, Inc., City Island,
    New York

FISH HAWK

A cruising cutter

To sit in the cockpit of *Fish Hawk* is to be surrounded by the functional beauty of wood. Her deck and cockpit platform are of teak, a wood so dimensionally stable that it needs no surface finish to keep it from shrinking or swelling, and so durable that it needs no coating to protect it from the weather. The oval coaming extends aft beyond the deck edge forming somewhat of a seatback for the passengers. It's made in two layers, the outer (not visible) runs horizontally and is bent to the shape of the curve, and the inner layer is made of vertical staving whose edges are splined together and whose exposed corners are delicately chamfered. A fitted rail cap covers the exposed seams and joints at the top of this structure.

For the helmsman, there's a seat atop the wheelbox—higher than the others for good visibility—with a hinged backrest that can be folded out of the way when the going gets rough. The engine controls lead to the wheelbox within reach, and the compass is mounted in a traditional brass binnacle, well protected from damage, yet within easy view of the helmsman.

Fish Hawk's cockpit is self-bailing; that is, its floor is above the surrounding water level and connected to the sea by means of pipes called scuppers that drain rainwater or spray back overboard rather than into the bilge of the boat.

LOA: 62'8"   Beam: 14'9"
Designed by John G. Alden
Built 1937 by Goudy & Stevens, East Boothbay, Maine
Photographed at St. Thomas, U.S. Virgin Islands, and
*   Newport, Rhode Island*

CHIPS

A P-class sloop

Some people called them floating lead mines; others sang their praises as being fast and fun to sail. Nowadays they're generally considered impractical. But there's little disagreement when looking at the boats themselves—and *Chips* is one of them—that they're supremely beautiful. I'm referring here to the low-sided, graceful, heavily ballasted racers that were built to the Universal Rule in the early 20th century. This rule, like other rating rules, handicapped boats through a time allowance so boats of differing design could race against each other fairly. Like the other rules, this one took into consideration key measurements, but it did so in such a way as to encourage beauty as well as speed. *Chips* is a P-boat, one of the "letter" classes designated under the Universal Rule, from J to S according to the boat's size. J-boats, the biggest, were the ones that competed for the *America*'s Cup in the 1930s.

With skillfully shaped overhangs and a low, graceful sheerline, *Chips* is a striking sight—and a rare one these days.

LOA: 50'3"   Beam: 10'3"
Designed by W. Starling Burgess
Built 1913 by the W. Starling Burgess Corp.,
*   Marblehead, Massachusetts*
Photographed at Noank, Connecticut

BELLE AVENTURE

An 85' Fife ketch

They say it's really tough to make an old boat look brand-new, but once in a while it happens as it did with the 85' Fife ketch *Belle Aventure*. She looks new all over, from her flawless, newly splined topsides to her impeccable teak deck. And her joiner-work and trim, above deck and below, have been made to look new not only by the usual refinishing but by carefully planing the worn corners to their former crispness and by working down other areas so they're perfectly fair. The wear of age is nowhere evident. McGruer's yard on Gareloch in Scotland, near where *Belle Aventure* was built more than 60 years ago, did the refurbishing in 1980 under the skill and good judgment of her captain, Paul Goss. New metal floor timbers, new butt blocks, and new chainplates were among the structural tasks carried out, and some accommodations changes were made as well. The main saloon, for example, was outfitted with new carpeting, upholstery, and brass lamps besides having its woodwork totally stripped and refinished. Chartering rather than private use is now *Belle Aventure*'s purpose; she has tastefully luxurious staterooms for six—that's right, only six—paying guests. Her regular crew numbers five.

LOA: 85'0"   Beam: 17'6"
Designed and built 1928 by Wm. Fife & Son,
    Fairlie, Scotland
Photographed at Newport, Rhode Island, and Antigua,
    West Indies

EILEAN

A 73' Fife ketch

Compared with pre-Depression days, there are but a handful of big classic sailing yachts in existence now. Of the few that survive and are kept up to proper yacht standards, most have to earn at least part of their keep by carrying passengers for hire. Although this is a more democratic way of life, it's not as bad as it may at first sound. The charterers, or (paying) "guests" as they're called, are given what once were the owner's quarters—obviously the most elegant to be had—while the present crew, even though one of them probably owns the boat, usually live in more modest spaces, perhaps in the fo'c's'le. These yachts are being used quite differently from what was originally planned. Nevertheless, everyone seems to win. The interiors of the yachts generally needed little changing for their new role and retain their classic layout and appearance, the charterers can indulge themselves in luxury for a week or so without the care or long-term expense of ownership, the owners make a reasonable living and can take pride in having a boat of their own and the fun of constantly sailing her, and there is money, interest, skill, and ambition to maintain these big, beautiful sailing craft in true Bristol condition.

LOA: 73'0"   Beam: 15'0"
Designed by W. & R.B. Fife
Built 1937 by Wm. Fife & Son, Fairlie, Scotland
Photographed in the Virgin Islands

LIMBAS

A Far East-built sloop

On a fine day, it's great to be in almost any boat in almost any place. But aboard a beautiful wooden boat, with a brisk northwest wind, and wild and aromatic Maine islands all around, life becomes about as good as it can ever get. Aboard *Limbas*, however, the crew (facing page) has turned its attention more to finishing the race than to savoring the scenery. Holding her steady in a puff as the lee rail momentarily goes awash, the skipper drives for the finish line less than a quarter-mile away. It won't be long now until the crew can enjoy the other pleasures of this special day. The annual Eggemoggin Reach Regatta is no ordinary race; it is an impressive gathering of 100 or so exceptionally lovely wooden sailing yachts in an exceptionally lovely part of the world. Just being there, admiring the boats at anchor and under sail, is such a treat that the racing itself often becomes secondary.

LOA: 45'4"   Beam: 10'6"
Designed by Sparkman & Stephens, Inc.
Built 1949 by Ah King Slipways, Hong Kong
Photographed at Brooklin and Blue Hill Falls, Maine

WHITE WINGS

A sloop built in Canada

Lean and slippery, yet large enough for comfortable accommodations, the Alden-designed sloop *White Wings* is an unusually fine boat. Below decks, the arrangement is particularly pleasing. As is evident, there is a jog in the aft end of the trunk cabin, an unusual feature that results from locating a good-sized owner's stateroom aft, between the cockpit and the main saloon. Bypassing the stateroom because of its placement, the companionway enters the main saloon directly. (The galley, out of the way near the mast, has connecting doors to the saloon and fo'c's'le.)

White Wings had a full racing crew the day the facing page photograph was taken, having just rounded the outer mark. At other times, if the self-tending, club-footed working jib were set, one or two people could sail her, and, once the sails were hoisted, there would be little for them to do but steer and enjoy.

LOA: 50'0"   Beam: 11'7"
Designed by John G. Alden
Built 1938 by J. J. Taylor & Sons, Toronto,
    Ontario, Canada
Photographed off Newport, Rhode Island

CHRISTMAS

A Burgess-designed double-ender

Double-enders, because they have similar buoyancy at both bow and stern, rise to oncoming seas better than boats with large transom sterns. Running off, double-enders are not thrown about as much; their pointed sterns allow the seas to ease past them gradually. No doubt about it, these craft have earned their reputation for being seakindly.

W. Starling Burgess, the designer of *Christmas*, was one of the all-time greats in his field, having been born, it would seem, with a natural talent for designing boats. An astonishing variety—from Gloucester fishing schooners to America's Cup defenders to forty-knot-plus craft for the military—came from the mind, eye, and hand of this creative genius. Fortunately, *Christmas* has an experienced owner who fully appreciates this pedigree. A thorough rebuilding, followed by sensible care, ensures this strikingly handsome double-ender an especially bright future.

LOA: 44'9"   Beam: 12'0"
Designed by W. Starling Burgess
Built 1931 by Eastern Shipbuilding Corp., Shelburne,
  Nova Scotia, Canada
Photographed off Mattapoisett, Massachusetts

RING-ANDERSEN

A charter ketch built in the Baltic

Who would have guessed when she was launched in 1948 as an ordinary power-driven freighter that this vessel would one day become the *ne plus ultra* of the Caribbean charter fleet? But her hull shape made a conversion feasible, and in 1962 she entered the trade, sporting a new ketch rig, a clipper bow, and passenger accommodations. Between 1980 and 1983, her heavy-timbered oak hull received an astonishingly complete rebuild, after which she was fitted and finished, inside and out, to yachtlike standards. She carries, with pride, the name of Denmark's Ring-Andersen Shipyard, which did both the original building and the recent rebuilding.

There's a crew of seven tending to the needs of only six guests, so passenger well-being is pretty much assured. Lucky are those who luxuriate aboard *Ring-Andersen*, but lucky too are we who can enjoy these splendid views of her.

LOA: 93'0"   Beam: 21'0"
Designed and built 1948 by the Ring-Andersen Shipyard,
      Svendborg, Denmark
Photographed at Antigua, West Indies

INDEX

Dimensions in this book represent the overall length and maximum beam of the hull proper.